INTO

THE

LIGHT

REAL LIFE STORIES
ABOUT ANGELIC VISITS,
VISIONS OF THE AFTERLIFE,
AND OTHER
PRE-DEATH EXPERIENCES

John Lerma, M.D.

NEW PAGE BOOKS
A division of The Career Press, Inc.
Pompton Plains, NJ

INTO THE LIGHT
EDITED BY JODI BRANDON
TYPESET BY EILEEN DOW MUNSON
Cover design by Dutton and Sherman
Printed in the U.S.A.

To order this title, please call toll-free 1-800-CAREER-1 (NJ and Canada: 201-848-0310) to order using VISA or MasterCard, or for further information on books from Career Press.

The Career Press, Inc., 220 West Parkway, Unit 12
Pompton Plains, NJ 07444
www.careerpress.com
www.newpagebooks.com

Library of Congress Cataloging-in-Publication Data
Lerma, John.
    Into the light : real life stories about angelic visits, visions of the afterlife, and other pre-death experiences / by John Lerma.
        p.cm.
    Includes bibliographical references and index.
    ISBN-13: 978-1-56414-972-5
    ISBN-10: 1-56414-972-2
        1. Near-death experiences—Anecdotes. I. Title.

BL535.L433 2007
133.901'3—dc22

                                                                    2007036199

*I would like to dedicate this book
in loving memory of
my father, John Lerma, Sr., and
my Great Aunt Eladia "Tia Lala" Rodriguez
for her kindness and unconditional love
on earth and now in the heavenly realm.*

*This book is also dedicated with total love to
my mother, Carmen Lerma, and children:
Daniella Lerma,
Mark Lerma,
and Ariana Lerma.
Four beautiful examples of God's love.*

Our love is with wholeness and interconnection;
Our separateness is but fear;
Our birth, our death, our birth;
And so goes this exhilarating play of God.

—John Lerma, M.D.

Contents

Preface

I'm often described as a high-energy individual, and most people want to know why I specialized in hospice and palliative medicine. Even my family could not figure it out at first. They said, "You spent all that time learning to heal people, and now you want to help them die?" Or, "Why would you want to spend so much time with people who are about to die, isn't it depressing?" Some people seem to think hospice doctors should be serious and talk in a soft voice, but those who are dying do not want that at all. They want to be treated the same as everyone else, as they are the same as everyone else. They want you to joke with them, laugh, and do silly things to amuse them and keep them engaged in life. The terminally ill yearn for these joyful attitudes, as they ultimately grasp the meaning of life and death, and an understanding that this phase of life should be celebrated and honored as the beginning of an awe-inspiring journey—a journey that leads us into the arms of our loving Creator.

During medical school, and as an intern, I had to contend with the onset of the AIDS epidemic, and it was devastating. The predictions for the infected population were dire. I gained great respect for the process of death during this time, and I wanted so much to help these souls complete their lives in a joyful way, instead of just trying to help them survive. It was excruciating at times to revive patients who I knew wanted to die, but were too incapacitated to express their wishes. I knew there had to be a better way to deal with the futility of this disease, as fighting tooth and nail and forcing patients to endure great pain, just to postpone the inevitable, was inhumane. After all, who were we trying to serve: ourselves or the patients?

Within a period of a few months, I witnessed an astonishing event that would later not only launch my career into hospice and palliative medicine, but ultimately reveal the answer regarding the futility of medical care. I was an intern working in a San Antonio hospital one full-moon night when a fatal head-on collision sent five patients to our emergency room. The victims were triaged and the youngest patients with the best chance of survival got the top doctors. For the interim, I was to care for patients with minor problems or patients with the least chance of survival. At that moment, Ricardo, an 82-year-old man, was brought in by the paramedics after collapsing at home during dinner. He was rushed into the trauma room, where I promptly initiated cardiopulmonary resuscitation. After the first shock, normal heart rhythm returned. Ricardo aroused slowly, mumbling something about "the light" and being out of his body. As I worked at stabilizing his heart rhythm, he continued to repeat the sentence "It felt like a roller coaster ride; it felt like a roller coaster." More alert now, he was able to communicate his symptoms, which included chest pain. I reassured him that pain medicine was given and told him not to worry. To keep him engaged, I asked him to tell me more about his roller-coaster ride. Ricardo replied, "I don't know what was happening except that I was flying over my body, and angels began to show me things I had done in my life." He looked at me, and with an elated smile said, "It was so beautiful. God and the angels told me I would survive this." Just after that brief conversation, he flat-lined and was shocked once more with no response. It was not until I injected epinephrine directly into his heart that a cardiac rhythm was obtained. He was rushed to the cardiac care unit where the cardiologists initiated several intravenous anti-arrhythmics in an attempt to stabilize his heart rate and rhythm. In the end, Ricardo had suffered a massive heart attack that responded well to the anti-arrhythmics, anticoagulants, and angioplasty.

While visiting the patients I had admitted the night before, I saw Ricardo waving and signaling to visit him first. I could not believe this man was awake, let alone alive. With a radiant smile that appeared to illuminate his whole countenance, he said, "Thank you for helping me." I told him I was so excited he had made a remarkable recovery. He said, "I owe it all to God. Dr Lerma, do you remember our conversation about the light and being out of my body?"

"*Of course I do,*" I replied.

Ricardo continued, "Well, I had a lot of realizations during that time. I guess you can say I negotiated with the angels and God to make things right with my family. You see, Dr. Lerma, I was abusive with my family and friends, and God gave me the opportunity to mend things with my wife." Mesmerized with his comments, I wondered about near-death stories I heard other doctors discuss and whether they were true or just the brain's response to sudden chemical and gaseous changes. In Ricardo's case, I was sure something miraculous had occurred, but there was no way of knowing. Completely enthralled, I continued my conversation with Ricardo, hoping there was something he would say that would prove his experience.

"Dr. Lerma, I need your help. I know you doubt my story, and in a way, so do I. That is why I need confirmation on whether this spiritual occurrence was real." Before I asked how that could be done, he said, "When I was out of my body and floating up above the trauma room I spotted a 1985 quarter lying on the right-hand corner of the 8-foot-high cardiac monitor. It was amidst the dust as if someone had put it there for this very reason. Dr. Lerma, could you please check for me? It would mean so much to me."

I was curious and skeptical enough to oblige him, and went to the emergency room with a ladder. I climbed up, with the nurses standing by. They were also curious to know if a patient had really been able to see something while we were bringing him back to life. We heard stories similar to that all the time, but there was usually no way to prove whether they had really seen something or just imagined it. To our total amazement, there it was, just as he had seen it, and even the year was right: 1985. There seemed no doubt that the only way he could have known it was there was if he placed it there himself or he saw it as he was floating up near the ceiling, as he described. Still skeptical, I wondered if this man could have put the quarter there, so I checked some of the details, and found there was no way he could have known the quarter was there. It had been years since he had been able to climb a ladder, and he had never worked in construction. I could find no connection with anyone who had worked on the newly built emergency trauma rooms. Was this confirmation that we exist beyond the body? At best, it piqued my interest in the death process, which, ultimately, led me into a career where stories such as this were a rule and not an exception.

This book is about ordinary people, in extraordinary situations, who selflessly shared their last days with me, knowing that their stories were going to bring comfort and peace to those who directly or indirectly heard the accounts of an all loving and righteous God. The heartfelt accounts of God's love as told by a 9-year-old boy, a murderer, a drug user, a Christian minister, an atheist, and a German Nazi are not only mystifying, but healing and uplifting. They all speak of the One God that creates with total love, forever reminding us that everyone on this planet serves a purpose and is unified from the same wholeness—a wholeness that will, in due time, create universal and eternal peace and love.

One patient's account reveals how unconditional love and random acts of kindness raise the level of humanity and spiritual growth for our planet and universe. Another patient explains that, as science and spirituality unite, many discoveries will be made, including a protein sequence in DNA that, when activated, will accelerate our progression to peaceful entities. Many of the visions and messages talk in depth about the need for self-love and self-forgiveness in order to have a loving earthly relationship and ultimately a peaceful transition back to God. Some of the people in the book had peaceful transitions and others difficult ones; nonetheless, the common denominator was their desire to provide further insight into the mysterious interface between life and death.

When I first began to reveal these stories as well as my personal research on the validity of pre-death visions, I faced criticism from and investigations by the medical community. I was compelled to continue my research as well as share the extraordinary tales of comfort and compassion; however, I did this at great peril to my career, truly believing that the messages these stories conveyed were instrumental in providing relief of both patients' and families spiritual, emotional, and interpersonal pain. The outcomes were simply astounding. Hence, the project of investigating pre-death experiences (PDEs) began. By the time *Into the Light* was written, I had successfully interviewed more than 2,000 terminally ill patients and recorded more than 500 pre-death experiences.

At my core, I am a scientist, and I did not come to the idea of angels and non-physical entities easily. I believed science had not done enough to narrowly define life, so I began with a skeptical view of the seemingly large number of supernatural occurrences that preceded death. When possible, I found a rational explanation and most often attributed the patients' visions to their advancing disease, medications, or a complete shutdown of body systems. Nevertheless, the similarity and sheer number of stories, as well as some unexplainable phenomena, began to weigh heavily in favor of something else. I do not attempt to define what that "something else" is, but simply recount the compelling stories of the terminally ill patients under my care.

The religious aspects of the stories come from the individuals and do not necessarily reflect my beliefs, for I am still observing and holding a place of scientific observation and skepticism while considering all of the possibilities. From a place of true compassion, I am presenting these heartfelt and spiritual experiences as inspiration and encouragement for the dying and the survivors of loss, and that includes all of us. My intention is to offer what I have observed and learned from the countless loving patients I had the honor of comforting, and that is the presence of hope, redemption, and unconditional love that exists at the end of our earthly journey. My hope is that the medical industry will embrace this information and gain new understanding of the dying process so as to focus greater attention on the spiritual needs of their patients as they leave this world.

The accounts in this book are of hospice patients during their last hours to days before making their final and most sacred journey. (Note that, although I use quotation marks to signify conversation between my patients, their families, and me throughout the book, they are actually a mixture of quotations from notes taken while interviewing patients as well as from my memory.) Most of the stories explore the mysterious realms of visions, synchronicities, prophecies, and the quantum field of infinite possibilities. Due to the unusually personal nature of the accounts, I have changed names and personal details. I hope you will enjoy and be uplifted by the amazing messages from the angels.

Introduction

The Last Days of Life

I n the last days of life, the terminally ill retreat within themselves as a way of preparing to release their soul. They tend to relive events in the distant past with varying feelings and often need help in obtaining closure. This is important to the timely release of the soul. During this time, the patient may stare intently at corners in the room, or have brief conversations with unseen spirits of deceased family members or brilliantly lit angelic beings. It is these spiritual beings that bring comfort and peace, and aid the patient in resolving unsettled emotional, interpersonal, and spiritual issues, with the ultimate goal of a peaceful transition to the afterlife. One may be quick to judge and openly discuss the patient's hallucinatory and delirious behavior, not realizing that these negative assertions dissuade the patient from openly discussing his or her spiritual experiences (which, ironically, only ends up prolonging the patient's suffering). To foster peace, family or friends should attempt at creating a secure and loving environment, free of criticism. This action allows the patient to describe his or her comforting visions as well as redemptive experiences, with the ultimate effect being the liberation of their emotional, interpersonal, and spiritual pain.

A strong desire to go home is expressed, even when the patient is at home. He or she may start speaking of needing to "catch the train," "catch the bus," or "fly home." These phrases are metaphors for the final and most sacred journey to heaven. The patient may reach upward as if attempting to feel the intangible. Many patients describe this reaching as an attempt to hold hands with their deceased loved one's or caress an "angel's wings." At this point, the spiritual beings are summoning the patient to walk towards them and *into the light*.

As evening approaches, delirium surfaces. The patient may begin picking or pulling off clothes, bedsheets, or intravenous lines or catheters. This is known as delirium, and is caused by a multitude of factors, including but not limited to pain, the inability to fully empty the bladder, constipation, dehydration, liver and kidney failure, fever, infection, low blood oxygen content, and, last but not least, the advancement of the disease process. Treatment varies and may include opiates such as morphine for pain and suffocation; a catheter for the release of retained urine; laxatives for constipation; intravenous or subcutaneous fluids for dehydration; oxygen via a nasal cannula or mask; and sedatives such as haloperidol, chlorpromazine, or, less often, lorazepam to provide rapid and lasting comfort.

At this point, the use of opiates and sedatives, whose main side effect is sedation, is usually necessary to comfort and protect the patient. The balance between relieving pain and maintaining cognitive awareness during the last few days of life will decrease dramatically, but with necessity. With the body's toxins elevating exponentially during the last few hours to days of life, this will further compromise one's ability to remain alert. One has to remember that this is the body's way of removing the patient's awareness of dying in order to protect the patient from the traumatic effects of the process. Families and friends would love to have their loved ones awake throughout the entire process, but the fact is that this would be too distressing for the patient.

It is imperative that family and friends allow the patient to sleep as often and as much as he or she desires during this last phase of dying. With the understanding that the hearing nerve most often survives the caustic processes of dying, family and friends, especially the patient, will find that brushing their loved one's hair lightly, moisturizing their dry lips and parched mouth, and providing soft verbal reassurances that all family and friends are united in love and in prayer, will bring him or her a sense of closure and peace. Continued encouragement to follow God's angels, as well as the patient's deceased loved ones, will assure a peaceful transition to the heavenly realm.

With a decreased level of consciousness, congestion of the lungs, a lack of palpable distal pulses, and cyanotic extremities, one is almost certain that death is hours away. During this time period, the patient has usually attained mind, body, and spirit closure, and is left feeling elated and exhilarated. Within minutes of departure from this world, one might notice one last tear and smile. This last tear is often termed *epihora*. Family and friends who have been intimately involved in relieving the patient's total body pain are sustained by an immense feeling of reassurance that their loved one was carried on the wings of angels to God's heavenly kingdom.

Chapter 1

Negotiating With Angels

It was one of those blindingly hot July days, dripping with humidity, when I pulled into Houston Hospice in my usual hurry. As I walked towards the hospice house, I took a moment to appreciate the serene gardens and breathe in the verdant beauty, as it seemingly emanated a sense of peace and love that was almost palpable. My pace suddenly slowed as I was now surrounded by gentleness, kindness, and perfect love. I had always sensed this love and peace radiate from the hospice facility, but never to this degree. I was about to meet wisdom and knowledge in the form of a blind 9-year-old boy with terminal cancer.

Matthew was not assigned to me. His usual doctor was unavailable to attend to him, so she asked if I could handle his admission to the inpatient care facility, the last stop for most terminally ill patients. I was happy to do it. I had heard that this was a very special 9-year-old boy, who had requested a transfer from home hospice to the inpatient unit so as not to cause further hardship on his family. I was curious to see what kind of child would do that. Walking toward his room, I skimmed through the hundreds of medical and surgical reports as well as the invasive and aggressive treatments Matthew had received over the last two years. I was in awe of how anyone, let alone this young, vibrant boy, could still be alive.

I took a deep breath as I entered his room and immediately felt a wave of compassion as I took stock of the ravages of his illness. Immediately I sensed there was something else present that drew my attention more strongly, something not visible, but palpable. A feeling? Energy? Wisdom? Courage? It was something familiar, but I didn't quite recognize it. I stopped for a moment, trying to identify the feeling, but Matthew heard or felt me enter the room, so I shook it off and introduced myself to put the family at ease. *"I am Dr. Lerma. Welcome. You must be Matthew,"* I said, intentionally directing my salutation to Matthew's sister, who was sitting directly opposite from Matthew.

When she started to laugh, Matthew protested loudly, "No, silly, I'm Matthew." Amazingly, he knew I had addressed her instead of him, considering he had been blind for more than a year. He smiled a magical crooked smile and began an animated attempt to make me laugh. "Dr. Lerma, I want to introduce you to Regina, my tumor. The doctors call her retinoblastoma and tell me she is a bad tumor, but I consider her my friend. You see, Dr. Lerma, Regina is going to help my family and other children who are sick."

"How is that possible?" I asked.

"Well, God's the only One that knows that, but all I have to do is accept her."

I told Matthew that I was so proud of him for wanting to help his family as well as so many people. I felt this was a coping mechanism, albeit one I had never experienced from a 9-year-old boy with an incurable and aggressive cancer to both his eyes. How could this fragile young boy, who was diagnosed only three years earlier, followed by the surgical removal of his eyes, with concomitant multiple rounds of chemotherapy and radiation, be so selfless and still without apparent worry? Was his spirituality the reason for his miraculous survival? "Soooo," Matthew said, sounding reminiscent of Dr. Freud, "you're not one of those seeerious doctors, are you?" I assured him that I was not, and the child blurted out excitedly, "I knew it. You're the one I've been waiting for. The one they told me about!" At that moment, I caught a movement in my peripheral vision and whirled around, thinking someone had entered the room, but oddly, no one was there. So I shook it off and asked Matthew what he meant by his last statement. He said a little cryptically and more quietly, "I'll tell you later. It's not time yet. It's a secret."

A tremendous amount of energy and joy radiated from this charismatic boy, and, as a doctor, I questioned whether he qualified for inpatient hospice care. It was apparent that Matthew was not as close to death as most patients who arrived at the inpatient facility, so I asked his mother why she felt he needed aggressive symptom management. With tears in her eyes and a shaky voice, she said, "He asked to be brought here because he didn't want to die at home. Dr. Lerma, I told him that God was going to heal him and was not ready for him, but no amount of persuading could change his mind. Matthew said his time was really close and that he did not want to burden his sisters and me with the difficult job of caring for him as he died. He is such a wonderful boy, always thinking of us, and watching out for us.

Matthew said he would be the kind of man that would always protect us. I don't know how he does it. I wouldn't have the strength to stay alive like he does. Dr. Lerma, you know I don't really believe in God, but I am starting to think that he was sent to my daughters and me from something greater than us all. Possibly God? Will you pray with me, Dr. Lerma?"

She was now crying inconsolably. Brushing a tear from my own eye, I put my arm around her and, softly but with fervor, prayed the only prayer I knew: the Lord's Prayer. In a piece-meal fashion, she recited the prayer along with me, and at its end, she looked at me square in the eyes and said, "Don't you feel it, Dr. Lerma? You know a presence of something wonderful and loving?"

"Without a doubt," I replied. *"Without a doubt."* I was truly inspired by what Matthew's mother had sensed.

Matthew's courage and strength, and ability to find joy during adversity, were astounding. I remember the physicians and nurses at the cancer hospital talking about how he radiated love and joy. They said that, despite his painful therapies, his constant smile, his beautiful, wise words, and his spontaneous heartfelt hugs always managed to make everyone feel loved. Medically, this fragile child, with a softball-sized tumor protruding from his right scalp, should have died months ago, slipped into unconsciousness, or have been in the throes of excruciating pain. Yet, he defied all the odds. Instead of an intolerant, resentful child, here was a joyful 9-year-old boy who had no problem holding clear conversation and an uncanny knack of making people feel happy. After a few visits, I noticed that I was not the only one captivated by Matthew's pure joy and infectious laugh. Everyone who had the pleasure of meeting him called him mature, delightfully funny, loving, compassionate, and wise beyond his years. Word of his alluring and charming personality drew families from surrounding rooms, often leaving them feeling profoundly moved. Incredibly, this sanguine, youthful spirit willfully accepted the life God had given him. As Matthew put it so eloquently, "My illness will bring my mom to Jesus Christ, and that is worth it!"

After Matthew's regular doctor returned, I felt the need to continue my visits. It was as if I was magically pulled into the room every time I passed the door. One day I asked Matthew how he had lived so long with all that he had endured. He seemed to be deciding if it was time to share this information. He cocked his head as if listening to someone talk, and then he said simply and matter-of-factly, "Okay, I'll tell him. Well, doc, it was a gift from God's angels." I was a little surprised by this revelation, but sometimes patients did mention angels, and I usually just ignored it as a side effect of the medications or the hallucinations of the dying mind. But this felt different somehow, as Matthew was very lucid and had refused all medications since his admission. Not wanting to jeopardize the relationship I had developed with Matthew by openly doubting his comments, I eagerly pursued the conversation by asking him what he meant by "it's a gift from God." He replied, "It's okay to tell you my secrets now. The angels just gave me permission to talk to you. I have lived this long because I asked my angels for extra time to allow my mother and sisters to accept my illness and death and especially to accept God."

"Why do you think your family needs all this help?" I asked Matthew.

"Dr. Lerma, my mother became very angry with God after my dad left us. She had no job, and my father did not help with money. She was angry with God. Then when they found my cancer, she lost her belief in God. She wondered why God was taking everyone she loved and at a bad time in her life. She stopped going to church, and my sisters followed my mom. I am going to help my mother and sisters. God has allowed me to stay until they are healed."

"Don't you want to be healed, Matthew?"

"In the beginning, yes, but now I know that, if I'm healed, my mom will not find God, and that is not good. I want to always have my mommy. So I am going to die to help my mommy find God. This way, I will have her forever. Do you understand, Dr. Lerma?"

"Oh Matthew, of course I do. I don't know what to say. I wish you could be healed and your mom find God too. Why can't the angels and God make that happen?"

Matthew replied, "Dr. Lerma, if you could see the other side, you wouldn't be asking me that question. You will see. It is all going to be perfect."

I was completely mesmerized by Matthew's astonishing revelations. How could his comments be construed as delirious? The clarity and clear understanding of his reasoning were beyond belief. I was now deeply captivated with Matthew's logic, and thus continued my conversations and delved further into researching the hallucinations of the dying.

Matthew continued, "The angels assured me that my family will find peace through Christ as a result of my faith and unconditional love for them." I could not believe the wisdom that was being imparted by this 9-year-old. Matthew said he had always believed in God's angels and had been conversing with them every Friday since he began chemotherapy. By this time, he knew that his illness had a purpose—a purpose to help his family and the world. I asked him how it would help the world, and he said, "Oh, you'll see how it works. The angels have plans for you, too, but that's still a secret." I couldn't drag any more information out of him, no matter how often I asked. I never knew a child who could keep a secret so well, but this was no ordinary child. The angels had chosen a worthy messenger.

What kind of child has the presence of mind to think so clearly about death, and to be so concerned for others when he is experiencing such trauma? And why did he request admission to our acute care center? What made him think he was about to die? How could he not be in excruciating pain with such a rapidly progressive, intra-cranial malignancy? These were questions that plagued me, and finally I decided to ask Mathew.

That same evening, when I got around to asking Matthew why he had requested admission for inpatient care, he confided, "I know my time is close, and I don't want to die at home. It would make my family too sad."

"*How do you know this*?" I asked.

As he glanced toward his mother, Matthew smiled and stated, "My angels told me."

This was the first time he had mentioned the angels in his mother's presence, and she looked completely shocked as she said, "You never told me that. Why didn't you tell me you were seeing angels?"

Again, as though it was as natural as rain, Matthew replied, "I wasn't supposed to tell you until now, but now it's okay to talk about them."

I pretended to whine as though I were a curious child, "*So what can you tell me about the angels?*"

Matthew grinned mischievously, and said, "Now that you ask, I can tell you a lot, but Dr. Lerma, first read me a short story, then I'll tell you more." He handed me a small children's book and told me to open it to page 24. As I searched for the page, I saw the simplicity of the stories and suddenly felt silly reading it to Matthew, as it was difficult to view him as a child. Yet, I felt it prudent to oblige him, and I cheerfully read the story aloud. It was obvious by now that Matthew had a knack for getting what he wanted; people just seemed to want to comply. The five-minute story he requested was about a little girl who kept a wonderful secret given to her by a fairy. The fairy told her that she could reveal the secret at a special time, and only at that special time. The importance of the story was veiled, but clearly evident. Matthew's mother and I both knew that his special time meant that death approached surely and steadily.

After the story, Matthew said the angels asked him to reveal the angelic messages, and that it was important to do it now. Mathew said, "I'll answer as many questions about the angels as they will allow." As a scientist, I set aside my clinical mind and opened my heart to this frail little angel messenger. My curiosity was piqued, and I eagerly began asking Matthew questions about life and God. He was clearly excited to be sharing his knowledge with regards to his disease and angelic experiences. Matthew told me, "Finally, I get to talk about all the cool stuff. Boy, it was hard not to tell anyone what I was seeing. Why don't we talk tomorrow? I am sort of sleepy right now."

"Absolutely," I replied. *"Any time you want to talk with me, just have the nurses page me. I don't care what time it is. I am here for you, Matthew. Remember: I love you."*

He smiled, gave me a warm hug and a kiss on my cheek and said, "Sleep with the angels, Dr. Lerma. I love you, too."

Matthew had me paged the following morning. He wanted me to talk and play with him. Surprisingly, I had an unusually low number of admissions that day, so I was able to spend all morning with him. Oddly, the next day was even slower, and in fact the entire week had been among the slowest in years. Was this just coincidence? Whatever it was, the extra time could not have come at a better time. As I entered his room, Matthew, without any pain or distress, asked me if I wanted to assemble Lego structures. *"Boy, that sounds cool. I always wanted a Lego set when I was young,"* I told him.

"Well, here's one. Let's go at it," Matthew commented. While playing, Matthew looked at me, as though he could see me, and said, "Okay, let's talk about the angels. Ask me some questions. I can feel your heart, and it has questions, so shoot."

I started the conversation. *"Are there any angels with us today, Matthew?"*

"Oh yes, they are here."

I looked around, but couldn't see anything, so I just kept talking. *"How many angels do you see?"*

"Three."

"*What color are they?*"

"They are bright gold."

"*How tall are they?*"

"They are a little taller than my favorite basketball player, David Robinson."

"*Do they come to you when you are sleeping or when you are awake?*"

"Both ways. They come in my dreams, and we all go swimming with the dolphins, seals, and penguins. It's a lot of fun. When I'm awake, they teach me things about the earth and people."

"*Can you tell me what they teach you about the earth and people?*"

"Yes. They tell me that the earth is sick like I am, and that the people have to learn to make it feel better so that everybody can be healthy and happy. Sometimes when I'm swimming with the dolphins and playing with Gabby, I can hear the earth crying because it is sick and is sad. It makes all of us sad. But Gabby has shown me what makes the earth laugh."

"*And what makes the earth laugh, Matthew?*"

"You make it laugh by swimming with the dolphins, seals, penguins, fish, and a bunch of other animals, and saying thank you to God for the water, plants, and all that stuff. Do you get it, Dr. Lerma?"

"*Boy, do I get it. Thank you, Matthew, for teaching me what I have forgotten with regard to respecting our planet and the animals God created for enjoyment and survival. By the way, Matthew, do your angels have names?*"

"Yes. The biggest one is Gabby, then Noe, and Raphy. They love us so much, Dr. Lerma."

I thought those were very strange names for angels, but then again, could those be nicknames for Gabriel, Noel, and Raphael? Was it possible that two of Matthew's angels were the Archangels the Bible spoke of? At that moment, a beautiful, young lady entered the room, and Matthew, looking elated, shouted out, "Hi, Mrs. Smith!" She and I looked at each other in total amazement, and silently wondered about his extrasensory perception. I immediately thought about what an opportune time it was to find out more about Matthew's social, emotional, and spiritual persona. Once again, without any prompting from my behalf, Matthew asked his teacher to recount a story that happened a few months earlier. It was this brief story that gave me a precise picture of who Matthew had always been. Mrs. Smith recounted:

> Matthew begged to go to school for show-and-tell day, and, although he was not in great shape to do it, the school wanted to help make him feel good in any way they could. All the kids showed up with that special something that would distinguish them from each other. Bubbly Susan brought her goldfish, little Jeff his fire truck, and Xavier even brought his loving mommy. In the end, it appeared that toys, animals, and even parents were the exhibits of choice. That was the case until Matthew was wheeled to the front of the classroom.
>
> Matthew said he wanted to show his tumor and talk about the golden ones. I was a little disconcerted because of Matthew's illness and was very protective of him, but he insisted that it was something he had to do. He said that he wanted to help the kids understand

that, just because somebody looks different or is sick, that they shouldn't be afraid or shut them out. He said they're just kids. I couldn't say no to him. To my surprise, he quickly had the kids laughing and asking question about being sick, and if the tumor hurt, and what it was like to be in the hospital. He mesmerized the whole room with his straightforward answers, punctuated by laughter and silly stories about the people at the hospital.

Then he told them that when he feels really bad that he goes to dreamland to a beautiful ocean and swims with the dolphins, holding on to their fins and riding on their backs while they jump out of the water. He told them if they ever get sick not to be afraid because God would send special angels to help them. He continued and said that angels are always with you and wanting to help; all you have to do is believe and ask. It was a defining moment for everyone in the room. Ever since then, I have to visit whenever I can. The amount of love and peace I get during my visits is awe-inspiring.

The teacher wiped her eyes as she reminisced, and I realized even more strongly that this was no ordinary boy. His love and concern for others allowed him to be of such great service to so many people. Before Mrs. Smith left, I asked her, as well as Matthew's mother, if they knew any children or people in Matthew's life with the names of his angels: Gabby, Noe and Raphy, as I still held a place of skepticism. Neither of them could remember any of his friends, schoolmates, pediatric patients, nurses, or doctors with those names. They were as perplexed as I was. Matthew was not exhibiting classic delirium or cognitive impairment as a side effect of either his cancer or medications. Were these visions and figures purely a coping mechanism? If so, how could this young boy, without eyes, accurately distinguish people's names and the color of their clothes? Did he have some sort of extrasensory perception, or was he truly obtaining information from unseen entities? I was having a difficult time reconciling what I was seeing with what I knew as a scientist. Either way, I was committed to continue helping Matthew find peace and comfort.

A day or two later, our conversation continued.

"How often do you see the angels, Matthew?"

He replied, "Every few days. Mostly on Fridays, I think."

"Why do you think they come on Fridays?"

"Because that's when I had my chemotherapy, and they want to help me feel better."

"Do they talk to you?"

"Sometimes."

"What do they say?"

"They ask me if I'm feeling okay."

"What do you tell them?"

"I tell them the truth—that sometimes I feel sick. They tell me they'll make me feel better whenever I feel bad. That's why I don't have any pain like you always think I should have."

"How do they make you feel better?"

"They show me blue water with dolphins and let me ride on them, and after that I feel better than before."

Matthew was confirming what he had told his classmates at show-and-tell, and now he was attributing it to the angels. It sounded wonderful, and I acknowledged that I would love to do that, too. He told me I could if I really wanted to. All I had to do is just believe and ask. I told him I really wanted to believe the way he did. He smiled and we continued.

"How does it feel to ride the dolphins?"

"I am soooo happy and laughing, and the dolphins talk to me, and the water and the sunshine all talk to each other. The angels tell me this is because they all have the one spirit of God."

"Wow. I'd like to hear them all talking to each other."

"Oh, you can if you really want to, and you will!"

"What else happens when you're there?"

"All my friends are there, too."

"Which friends?"

"The little kids that were sick with me at the hospital."

"Have they already died?"

"Most have, but some are just visiting during their treatment."

"What do the kids tell you?"

"They they're so proud of me and they'll come back for me really soon."

"How soon?"

"Really soon."

"Are there children in the room with us?"

"No, they only come on Friday."

"Do you ever wish you could get better?"

"Yes, sometimes."

"Can't the angels make you well?"

"They could, but they showed me the things that made me choose to be sick. They said they'd make me well if I wanted, but I'm trying to help my family, and that's more important. When people volunteer to suffer for others, it changes the lives of the people you suffer for. Even from my bed I'm able to help so many people."

"I know. I can see that you're helping me right now."

Matthew felt how moved I was by this. He put his hand on my arm and said, "Don't be sad. If you could see what I see—and you will one day—you'd be really happy for me."

There it was again: that cryptic language. I cleared my throat, pulled myself together, took a deep breath, and continued, *"What things should I tell my patients who are dying?"*

Matthew replied, "Tell them to say 'I'm sorry' for hurting others and also to say 'I'm sorry' to God. God wants us to believe in His Son who died for our sins. He wants us to be good and when we do wrong to try to do better and to always remember He loves us so much and wants us to love ourselves like He loves us. If we love ourselves, then we can love others and the world can be happy. The angels told me that this is not far way."

That was powerful advice. I thought about how I could use it in my own life, and what a difference it would make if I just did that one little thing. All I could think of was the simplicity of his message, and how often we fail at giving others and ourselves a break. Yes, this little boy was teaching me things I never learned in medical school.

On Friday, at around four in the afternoon, I stopped in to see if Matthew had any new messages from the angels. I was fascinated by our conversations, and, even though I had a busy schedule, I still felt compelled to make time to talk to this little sage in a broken body. Matthew smiled when I entered the room. I could not help but be captivated with the fact that this sightless young boy always knew who I was, as well as most people who entered his room.

I gave him a hug, and we continued our angel dialogue.

"Do you mind if I ask you more questions about the angels, Matthew?"

"No."

"Do you know today is Friday?"

"Yep. The angels were here in the morning. They woke me from my sleep."

"What did they say?"

"They asked me how I was feeling."

"What did you tell them?"

"I said I'm feeling sleepy and very happy."

"Why are you so happy?"

"Because I was swimming with Jesus, the angels, the dolphins, and my friends. Jesus came and played with all of us today and told those of us who were sick that we were no longer going to hurt or be sad. He was going to have his angels pick us up from our hospital beds and take us to play with the dolphins, my friends, and anything we desired forever."

"Is this the first time that Jesus has played with you and your friends?"

"You're so silly. Of course not. Don't you see that HE was the dolphins, the water, the sky, and everything else? HE is what was making me laugh and giving me the choice to help myself, my family, and others."

Feeling completely emotionally disarmed, I continued the heartfelt conversation. *"So Matthew, what else did Jesus and the angels say?"*

"Well, Jesus said that my time here with my mom and sisters is going to end, and that my wish is going to come true. Raphy then said that my mom and sisters will be happy for where I'm going, and that Jesus, our God, and all of us angels are going to take care of them forever."

"So, do you really think your cancer was to help your family and other people?"

"Yes. It feels so right."

"So, will I know the angels' secrets someday?"

"Yes, they said they'd come to you when you're like me."

"Will I be sick with cancer?"

"No, just sick, and they said I could come back to be with you, too."

At that moment, tears rolled down my face, and I hugged this special child of God, because I finally knew that the things he was saying were true. I told him, *"Thank you for being such an honest, kind, wonderful patient and friend."* Matthew did not know that I was dealing with my own health challenges, but apparently the angels did. This convinced me that the information Matthew was providing was true. Matthew hugged me back and whispered in my ear, "The angels are going to pick me up on Monday. Will I get to see you before then?"

"Of course," I assured him. *"I wouldn't miss it for the world, Matthew. I want to put this in a book and let people know about your story. Do you mind?"*

"No, the angels told me to talk to you so you could do that."

"What else do they want you to tell me?"

"To tell people that angels are real and they really care about us and want to help us. They want us not to be scared and to pray to God always for help like I did."

"What do you want to tell the world?"

"Not to be scared of dying when you believe in God. It's actually pretty fun, with lots of people, dolphins, and angels that make you laugh. I told the dolphins it must be fun to be dolphins, and they said it must be fun to be a young kid, too. Isn't that funny? We all want to be something else."

I made my visit to Matthew early Monday around seven in the morning, because that is when Matthew said the angels would visit. When I entered, I heard Matthew laughing with his sisters while playing the karaoke machine. Matthew knew the moment I arrived and said, "Hello again," as if he could see. As they were singing, I joined in for a moment and then said, in my best DJ voice, *"Goooood morning, everyone. How is Matthew feeling today?"*

"Great! I slept great, and I don't even have any pain." I started to ask if the angels were in the room, but before I could get the words out, Matthew boldly spoke up. "Dr. Lerma, do you know there are about 20 angels in the room with us right now?"

"Really? Anyone else?" I asked.

"Yep, all my friends from the beach. It's like a big party with hats and balloons and everything. They're all laughing, and the angels are so bright and gold that the light makes everyone in the room look gold, too. All this light makes me feel like when I was in the first grade when I could run and play all day in the sunshine." Matthew's words filled his mother and sisters with an incredible joy and sadness. His mother prayed aloud into the karaoke machine, saying, "God, I'm ready to give him back to you now. I don't want him to suffer anymore. I love you, Jesus. I want to thank you for letting us feel the love from my son for as long as we did. But please, don't make him suffer for us anymore."

After her prayer, Matthew, with a look of exhilaration, turned towards me and said, "It's done."

"What's done?" I asked.

"My wish is granted. My family opened their hearts to Jesus." Matthew then gifted me with his final words: "I'll see you later." The little boy nodded his head as if he was sharing a special secret that only I would understand. I knew he meant that he would be by my side upon my death.

It was about four in the afternoon when Matthew went to sleep and slipped into a coma. Matthew passed away peacefully at six in the evening with his family at his bedside. I was sure his friends and angels took him home. Matthew's mother and sisters sat there for a long time just looking at his peaceful face with the crooked smile still on it. I could feel his spirit still around, no longer in the worn-out body. I could see that Matthew's mother was finally at peace with her son leaving. I knew that this world was a better place for Matthew having been here, even if only for a few years.

Everything had happened exactly as he said it would. As I left the room for the last time, I could swear I heard the sound of dolphin laughter and children giggling in the distance while water splashed in the background. But of course, as a doctor, I wouldn't say that's true. I can only honor the memory of what a little boy said about the angels on his way out. Interestingly, in my dreams I now swim with the dolphins regularly, and occasionally see Matthew there, more radiant than ever.

Doctor's Notes and More Dialogue With Matthew

After Matthew was gone, I kept thinking about our conversations. As a doctor, especially a hospice doctor, it was challenging for me to believe and understand the concept that suffering serves a real purpose in the world. I've heard from patients over and over again that their willful suffering is part of their learning experience—that it serves other people as well as themselves. I am still grappling with that concept, but now I try to use the time at the end of a patient's life to learn about their spiritual insights so I can share it with others as the wisdom of dying. Here is some more information Matthew provided in response to my questions for the angels. I hope you will consider them in the spirit with which they are shared.

"What is heaven?"

"Well, I know it feels like it's your birthday all the time, and the gifts are so much better. All you have to do is take Jesus' hand and He will take you home."

"Does everybody see that?"

"Yes, but only when they believe in love. You know that love is God."

"Is heaven like earth?"

"Yes, but it's perfect. It's like earth, but we finally get to live our lives without worry and have everything we want. When you finally get really done with all toys and things, you understand it's nothing, and you move on. The angels say we move toward thought at that time. I'm not sure what that means."

"Why would heaven be like earth?"

"Why not? It is really a wonderful creation of God that He wants us to really love. There is so much more, Dr. Lerma. For me, I like to swim with the dolphins because they talk to me and I talk to them. I tell them how wonderful it is to be a dolphin, and they tell me how wonderful it is to be a kid. And all the trees talk, and the water. Everything seems to talk to you and make you feel so happy."

"Why do you have three golden angels?

"You start out with one, and you get more when you're really sick. During the last three to four days, you might have 30 to 40 angels—as many as you need to feel good about leaving your family and going with God."

"Do they all look like these golden angels?"

"No, there are different kinds. Some are brighter and bigger, some are smaller."

"Why?"

"They have more power and they can do different things." Laughing, he said, "It's like our president, the senators, and then my mommy."

"What happens when we die?"

"When we leave this body and go with Jesus, we do that one great thing we always wanted to do, but were not able to do. We are learning things here on earth about love, and it continues in heaven with God. You just sort of move on to the next grade, and you step forward where you left off. God has so much planned for His children. I hear it's better than anything on earth. We can't do things here on earth because most of us don't believe we can do it. We just need to know that. That's just the basics. You could do the same things on earth if you believed enough. The angels told me it's like the Peter Pan story. It's very simple, Dr. Lerma."

"What about evil? Is there such a thing?

"There are bad things in the world, but we are all responsible, and we can change it, and that is the goal of God and our goal, too: to make the changes. Jesus told me to just believe in Him and to believe in ourselves, and that one day soon all dark things will turn to a happy light. I saw part of God's plan and it's wonderful. Dr. Lerma, just know that all the horrible things that are happening to all of us are because of the body and our mind. It is up to all of us, especially those with healthy lives, to use our minds and hearts to teach about Jesus' love for us and to depend on God to help us find cures for the world's diseases of the mind and body. It will become easier as more and more healthy people are being born with the answers to our problems and with a love for God. Those people who hurt and kill people are very sick and need not be judged but helped, especially through prayer. God wants us to depend on Him and work together to reach His plan. Please tell everyone you meet,

Dr. Lerma, of the good news that Jesus died for every bad thing we have done and will ever do, and that He has the answer to the world's problems. By believing in Him, we will find health, peace, and love. We should always pray for peace and love and then try to do things, including work, which makes you truly happy. This will make you happy, peaceful, and loving, and everyone around you. Through this peace and love, sadness, sickness, hunger, wars, and much more will be gone one day."

"So, it's all in prayer and in believing in Jesus Christ?"

"Yes, just believe in Jesus. Then listen to Him. He and the angels are always talking to us and trying to keep us happy and safe. Listen to that feeling in your heart first. Not your mind first. The mind without the heart leading it is dangerous. Learn to listen to God. He really wants to help, but not control us!"

Chapter 2

The Smile

Jacob was a beautiful little boy, with wild, curly black hair and pale skin. Upon meeting him, I saw a frail, 2-year-old who resembled a little rag doll. He was unable to move or open his eyes. He could not cry, swallow, or even smile any longer. When Jacob lost his smile, his parents knew his soul was gone. He had such a beautiful smile, and then, overnight, the disease invaded his facial nerve, leaving his facial and respiratory muscles paralyzed. His mother cried as she recounted that terrible day. Jacob had to be put on a life support after that. She said that, after being born, he developed normally for the first year. Just before his second birthday, he exhibited signs of muscle wasting and began to quickly regress and degenerate. His illness reduced his muscles to jelly, leaving him in a flaccid state, unable to express his pain.

It was heart-wrenching and heartwarming to watch this family try to make its little boy's last days peaceful and filled with love. His mother rocked him, sang to him, and massaged his little body. She kissed his forehead sweetly every time she entered and left the room. His older brother, Michael, who was only 4 years old and full of energy and life, did not seem to understand why Jacob slept all the time and couldn't play with him. He sat for hours on the bed next to Jacob reading him books (or at least that is what he called it). They were mostly picture books, but Michael told excellent stories about the pictures, and he never tired of talking to Jacob as he played on the floor next to the bed.

After spending more than four months at the hospital on life support, Jacob's parents could no longer watch him lie there and slowly decline. The doctors assured them that he had no possible chance of recovery and repeatedly recommended him to hospice. After several opinions from multiple pediatric neurologists and geneticists gave no hope of recovery, Jacob's parents finally consented to comfort care. He was discharged to home hospice care, as the family wanted him to be surrounded by all his stuffed animals and the comfort of home. The next few weeks were quite difficult for Jacob's mother, father, and brother. With the daily education and support from the pediatric hospice nurse, aid, and chaplain, the family was able to cope.

During one of my visits to their home, Jacob's mother asked me if I believed in heaven. I replied, *"Yes. Why do you ask, Sarah?"*

"Well, I was contemplating our traditional Jewish belief that souls go to a place called She-ol, a dwelling place of all deceased where they wait for their Messiah to resurrect them. There are many Jews nowadays who have varying beliefs, including Messianic Jews, who hold the Christian heavenly principle. I love my religion, but I want him to go to heaven, so he can run and play and do those things he was not able to here on earth. He deserves that. He's just an innocent little baby. I spoke with the Rabbi, and he said that I can pray for that. What do you think, Dr. Lerma?"

"I understand your pain and desires for your little one, and I agree with your Rabbi that prayer is powerful." I remembered what Matthew had told me about prayer and about sharing his story, so I told Sarah about Matthew and his mother, and their spiritual experiences. Amazingly, she was comforted and touched by the stories of hope, and began praying to God for a sign to let her know that her little Jacob would be with Him and the angels.

The next day, I shared more of Matthew's story, with Michael, Sr., Sarah, and little Michael, and spoke further of Raphy, Noe, Gabby, and the dolphins, and they all seemed to be engulfed with peace and comfort. At that moment I also felt a wonderful sense of tranquility and was grateful to the little boy with the crooked smile.

Within minutes of finishing the tale, Jacob opened his eyes, smiled really big, and raised his arms as if he was reaching for someone above him. I was stunned. It was impossible for him to rally that kind of muscle strength. He smiled, his arms ascended, and then he died. His mother was sitting on the bed, and she was too shocked to cry or say anything at all.

Michael had been playing on the floor and, when Jacob died, he stood up and walked towards the bed next to his mother. As he was about to sit next to his mother, he abruptly stopped, and went around and sat on the other side. Curious, Sarah asked him why he moved to the other side of the bed. Michael quickly replied, "There is an angel sitting next to you, so I couldn't sit there. Don't you see him, Mom?" She looked flabbergasted, but she felt comforted by her little son. Michael suddenly touched his brother's body and ran out the door crying. Before we could go to him, he turned around and calmly walked back with tears still on his face. He walked up to his little brother and lifted his arm. His mom asked what he was doing. He said, "They are right."

"Who's right, sweetie?" his mother asked.

He answered, "The angels. They're in the hall with Jacob, and they told me his body is just a shell. They told me to come and see for myself. They are right." He lifted the Jacob's arm again and let it drop. "It's just a shell. Jacob is with the angels." Michael said Jacob was smiling, laughing, and doing somersaults in the hallway. Sarah and Michael looked at me, with both questions and hope in their eyes.

I said, "You both prayed for a sign and you were given more than one. Jacob smiling and lifting his atrophied arms was alone miraculous. Also, 4-year-old children have no concept of death, and your 4-year-old is telling you what the angels have revealed to him. I think that's a big sign." Sarah and Michael started to cry, thanked me, and hugged little Michael. It was such a beautiful and poignant moment.

 ## Doctor's Notes

Later, Sarah recounted the story to her Rabbi, and he had her repeat it to the congregation. Finally, that gave her a sense of acceptance and closure, and a realization that her son was truly with the angels, not sleeping and waiting. She was so happy with that reassurance. Little Michael continued to tell stories of Jacob coming to play with him for the next year or so, and he said the angels would "fly him in and out." That was further encouragement for their mother, which allowed her to demonstrate a deeper love to Michael.

Chapter 3

A Change of Heart

Leon was a 78-year-old Baptist minister with stage-four colon cancer. When he arrived at the inpatient unit, he was in dire need of pain management and hydration. As his functional status declined, so did his ability to eat or drink. Despite his fading physical strength, though, his spiritual vigor intensified, allowing him to impart varying religious and spiritual messages.

Two days after his admission, I noted that he was focusing at the corner of the room, where earlier patients had alleged to see angels. Curious, I asked him what he was concentrating on. He scanned me suspiciously and said, "What do you want to know?" I asked if he was seeing anything unusual. "Like angels?" he replied.

"*Yes*," I answered.

"Totally. Do you want to know more about that?"

"*Absolutely.*"

"Well, let's just see if I'll be around long enough to tell you what I'm seeing and learning. As far as quality time, I don't think that will be a problem."

"*I'm not sure what you mean*," I explained.

With tears in his eyes, Leon responded, "You see, my family is very busy and the time they spend with me is infrequent and, when they do visit, it's swift. So, why don't you come back when you're done visiting your patients, and I'll tell you more. I suppose this can be a time of expansion for both of us." We both smiled, and gave each other a warm hug. It was quite evident to me at that moment that Leon had opened his heart and knew I would not abandon him.

Later that afternoon, I returned as promised, and Leon began to share his wisdom. He had lived his life as a hard-line Christian fundamentalist with many prejudices and judgments against what he called the misguided and the heathens. He actively organized nationwide protests against gay marriages, and he worked to convince homosexuals that they were possessed and needed exorcising. He truly believed he was doing God's work and pursued it with a vengeance. If he ever questioned his beliefs, he rebuked his doubt and found Bible verses to bolster confidence in his actions. He was an old-time preacher full of hell-fire and brimstone. He liked to say to fellow ministers, "None of this *wishy-washy, feel-good crap* spouted by today's young preachers. The truth is the truth and it hurts." He had lived most of his life around this philosophy. Now, at the end, he couldn't explain everything that was happening, but it was changing him profoundly.

Although he was a devout Bible-based Christian and re-called reading stories of angels appearing to people, he didn't really believe that angels appeared to people in this day and age. He thought they were delusional people that *the enemy* had fooled into false beliefs. He discounted near-death experiences as hallucinations provided by Satan and did not believe it was possible to have an out-of-body experience. Throughout his ministry, he claimed to have cast demons out of psychics, mediums, and astrologers by convincing them that they were working for the dark side. He was powerfully persuasive and put the fear of God into several generations of worshippers throughout his 50-year ministry.

When the first angel came, Leon felt it was Satan coming to tempt him. But as the experiences continued, he came to recognize and accept the loving presence of God in everything that was happening. "I was allowed to talk to angels and to other people with knowledge of life and the afterlife, and I was allowed to talk with God," Leon told me. I was awestruck. I had heard many stories, but I had not heard many people say they had been allowed to talk directly with God. I asked him about his conversation with God. He answered, "All in good time. I want to tell my story the way I experienced it." Fascinated to hear more, I clammed up and let him continue.

"One of my first conversations with the angels was about women, and how important Mother Mary is. In Baptist theology, Mary's role is not emphasized, and women are admonished to subjugate themselves to their mates."

He continued, "That's how I felt about women, and that's how I treated my wife; she was my possession. I never really loved her deep in my heart. I married her because she was a good Christian woman and would make a good preacher's wife. In fact, I was in love with another young woman before I got married, but she was not of my faith. I felt we could never be married since we did not share the same beliefs." The angels showed him that Mary was an incredible woman, full of love, and, as Jesus did, she ascended into the heavens. They told him that he should have loved and honored his wife as if she were Mary, the mother of Jesus. They said, 'Every woman and every mother is just as important and sacred as Mary.'"

He shook his head and said, "I felt remorse for the coldness my wife had to put up with and understood why my wife's visits were infrequent. After that, they showed me what my life would have been like if I had married the woman I really loved. They showed us being happy and playing with our children, camping, fishing, and taking trips to Disneyland." His depression worsened as he contemplated his decisions in life. "I never had much fun with my children because they were a constant reminder that I married out of a sense of duty to my church and not the true love God had offered me. I raised my children with discipline but not much affection. They showed me times when my children were begging for an expression of love, but I turned away and threw myself into my church. I soon realized how cold my heart had grown because of my wrong choices. I discounted the value of love, even though the Bible says our greatest gift from God is love. I just pretended it wasn't important. It was too painful to face the truth. When I allowed the angels to guide me during my life review, I cried inconsolably. I knew I could have been blissful if I had just listened to my heart and released my flawed ideas about what God wanted from me. My life would have been so much more fulfilling."

He paused for a moment, glanced at me, and, when I kept silent, continued. "They showed me what a powerful ministry I would have fashioned, if only I had opened my heart and poured love on my congregation instead of condemnation. They reminded me that God is love and His love transcended all boundaries. I felt like a failure, but they assured me I wasn't. The angelic messengers revealed how my family had indoctrinated me into duty over love, especially my father, who had passed it on to me through his behavior." He shook his head sadly and commented, "I can remember wanting my father to play with me, but he was too busy earning a living. He was always too busy for me. The little boy in me cried out in pain when I remembered this long-repressed desire, and the angels held me in their arms and let me cry until I was able to understand the message. It felt as though they had held me for a lifetime. Once I developed clarity, they stroked my hair and sang sweet songs until I was at peace. The intensity of their love was overwhelming."

Leon continued his angelic messages: "All of us on earth reached our last intellectual enlightenment more than 50 years ago, which resulted in our current life in technology and science. This critical mass, as well as others in the past and future, has provided and will provide us with the necessary knowledge to free ourselves from our basic survival issues and expand us towards peace and love. God is currently gracing us with another enlightenment period. This time it will only involve love and spirituality, because man failed to factor in spirituality to the technological and scientific knowledge given during the last period. It will be a daunting effort to stop the destruction of humanity and knowledge by the raw power of technology and science that man's irresponsibility has unleashed. The ability to overcome our adversity can only be attained by invoking His grace, and believing in the power of prayer first, then action. This will assure our continued growth and survival as children of God."

I felt a strong wave of resonance with what he was saying and asked for further insight into prayer and action on evading our destruction. He said, "It's simple, but not easy to accomplish in this day and age. We can avert it through joy, prayer, and knowledge, and just by being joyful and showing love to everyone in our lives. Just remember that God will continue granting us countless chances to correct our wrongs so all souls will have the opportunity to experience His Son's teachings of unconditional love and peace."

The next afternoon, Leon was eager to tell me the difference between near-death experiences and his personal visions. As soon as I sat at the end of his bed, Leon said, "Here we go. What we know about God and the afterlife is from people and their accounts of out-of-body and near-death experiences and the writings of the church. During a near-death experience, the angels, God, or deceased loved ones talk to the person who's out of his body. What I am doing right now is slightly different. I am awake, talking to you, and still able to hold conversations with the angels. I'm completely connected to both sides at once."

"*Hmm*," I said. "*So, you could say this is like a pre-death experience or a death bed experience.*"

He chuckled and said, "I guess you could say that. Anyway, the experience is so real that, at one point, I was questioning whether I was dreaming, hallucinating, or delirious." I reassured him that he was not exhibiting the classic signs of delirium. I explained that patients with delirium have hallucinations of objects, the environment and people who are still alive. They are not able to hold meaningful conversations and recall the experiences at a later date. "It wasn't until the events the spiritual beings showed me came true that I became convinced that what I was experiencing is real, and what I am being told is true. My final validation came when you told me several stories about other patients' spiritual experiences that were almost exactly like mine. I could finally trust myself again. Thank you for that," he said. I smiled and nodded as I squeezed his hand. He never quite got around to describing heaven or the other side, and I'm pretty sure he never intended to reveal that to me.

There was another very important lesson Leon wanted me to share. His angelic teachers showered him with the infinite knowledge and true power of the Bible, and for the first time he understood all the lessons and knowledge that were being missed because of our willful and narrow perspective on creation. He said the information we have extracted from the Bible to date is just the tip of the iceberg. The amount of lessons, knowledge, and prophecies the Bible holds is similar to DNA's potential information.

Leon noted, "When man collectively opens his mind to the infinite teachings of the Bible, then God will make His second return."

"Did the angels tell you this?" I asked.

"Definitely." I was completely mesmerized by that statement. Could this be true? If there were many untapped messages in the Bible, then what could they be? Leon said he was not allowed to reveal any part of those teachings, because that could affect our lessons and affect man's desire to seek the one truth: God.

Leon wanted to remind me that every Bible study needs to be taught with an open heart and mind with allowances for interpretation. He continued, "The responsibility I had as a preacher was to teach God's Word, but throughout the years, and depending on my mood, I used the pulpit for my own ends. I manipulated it to preach my own belief system, and I regret that now. Today's society feels that scholars and theologians have deciphered the entire meaning of the Bible, but that is so untrue. When mankind awakens spiritually, the total knowledge and understanding of God's Word will be revealed. The key is being spiritual and not solely religious."

He sighed deeply and shook his head. "We get over-invested in our beliefs and find ways to enforce them through the Word. We don't have broad enough knowledge and wisdom to understand what God is really telling us. For instance, I was so prejudiced against gays, and so adamant that God would condemn them, but the angels showed me a different way of looking at that issue. The angels said that God never makes mistakes. Every human being desires love, and it's not for us to determine who they are going to love. If someone can love them back, then that's perfection." He understood it for the first time, and that was an issue that had weighed on him heavily because he preached near the Montrose area, a predominantly gay community. Leon had chosen to preach there as a protest to the lifestyle that he felt was contrary to Christian teachings. He held all kinds of protests against gays. "Now," Leon said, "I know I am dying, and when I start to become worried and terribly fearful, the angels fill me with their healing love. There were angels who look like men, and I loved them back. It was incredible; love is perfection, and for us to judge that love denies God's incredible truth. When the angels opened up my dark side and my fears, I realized that I have always feared being in love. I did not marry my true love, and I always carried that lack of love within me. Dr. Lerma, it was that repressed desire for love that led me to judge love in all its forms. Incredible, how intricate our minds are."

He took a deep, raspy breath and kept talking. "The angels showed me that even in gay relationships, there is a male and female coming together. One person will always be holding the masculine, and the other will be holding the feminine." I agreed with him and told him that, as a doctor, I know that we are just beginning to understand the chromosomal truth about feminine and masculine attributes. It's not just the phenotype that determines the *whole* person. He said, "That's the kind of thing the angels were trying to tell me. As our scientific understanding expands, and we integrate that knowledge with understanding, we will gain new understanding of God's Word. The Word was there all along, but we just didn't understand the full meaning."

He also talked about the dangers about using the all-or-none mentality to interpret principles taught in the Bible, Qur'an, or Torah. "For instance," he said, "the biblical parable that articulates if you have the faith of a grain of mustard seed, you can command that mountain to move, and it will move. Some people may take that to mean that if it does not happen, we don't have enough faith. That was how I operated: through guilt. I told people, 'You can heal yourself, and if you can't you're doing something wrong, or God is punishing you, or He is trying to teach you a lesson.' I was shown how much harm that does to people and how destructive guilt is. I was also shown how much good encouragement does." He continued, "The parable of the mustard seed is really about physics, mathematics, deeper thought, and how it can create. Literally you can make that mountain move, but you have to understand that it works through love. If one doesn't have love, one will not understand its deeper meanings. I know I didn't."

He paused a moment, as if listening to the other side, and then said, "Just think: If we were only using 10 percent of our brain, that would be almost three times what most people are using. Even Einstein used less than 10 percent. So, we are interpreting the Bible using about 3 percent of our brain. Imagine that." He laughed. "How can we interpret God's Word through such a small filter? One must allow the Holy Spirit to enable that process."

His love was so intense that it was almost palpable. I was so elated that he had found his true love for the first time. In total exhilaration, he continued to preach his final and most glorious sermon. I was happy to listen and take in all that he was saying. "As we progress, we understand more and more about what God is communicating through the Bible. Look at Joel Osteen. I never enjoyed his sermons because he was too positive and encouraging for me. I guess it's because I really wanted to feel positive like him. I know his secret. He is in love with Victoria, his wife! Wow! Look at what his true love brought him: multiple and multiple blessings. Joel has the faith of a mustard seed and he made mountains move in the name of Christ! There are definite generational blessings, as there is generational sin. Dr. Lerma, don't you see how Christ's true love can be passed on to heal and create? Joel's mother was healed of cancer, and Joel created a worldwide ministry."

"Yes I do, Leon. Yes, I do."

Leon continued, "Joel talks about creating through our words, and he's touching something within large numbers of people. He refers to the Bible, but he uses only one or two verses for a whole sermon. That's all he needs. You see, Joel Osteen is what we are moving to. The judgment days are over. There are more people in this world now that want to forgive and live in peace, but the judgers have had the money, the power, and the fortitude to make things happen. It's changing now. It's a done deal. God is not going to allow that to continue. In the next five hundred to one thousand years, the Word of God will be interpreted very differently." Leon said, "Look at me, I'm obsolete. That's why its time for me to go now." He suddenly turned to look at the clock and, with a big smile, said, "I love you, Dr. Lerma. And with true love. I will always be with you, my friend. By the way, the angels are going to give me what I asked for: time to apologize to my wife and children and to show them the unconditional love I should have had for them. The angels told me that, through my suffering and desire to learn about God's love, my wife and children will obtain an inheritance of generational blessings."

For the next three days, Leon's wife and children spent countless hours listening to his angel stories. On the fourth day of demonstrating his undying love for them, Leon fell asleep for the last time and gently departed this world.

Doctor's Notes
and More Dialogue With Leon

It was interesting to me that the angels shared so much scientific information with a man who had no science background. Nonetheless, much of what he talked about was cutting-edge. With regard to his comments on homosexuality, neuroscientists are currently examining the pineal gland and its function on sexual attraction. There is a possibility that the gland may even hold information on what sex we are beyond the chromosomal level. The fact that these studies are in process, and not general public knowledge, may lend credence to the minister's revelations. It makes sense that, no matter what genetic abnormalities there maybe with regard to sexual preference, the one element that is not affected is the basic attraction of the masculine to the feminine. Maybe that's what God meant when He spoke about man and woman.

I was impressed with the concept that, when we desire complete knowledge and can comprehend it, the hidden wisdom of the Bible will be revealed, and its unfolding will never end because we can never know everything that God knows. Leon told me that God foresaw our mental, emotional, and spiritual progression towards a strong desire to know more about His Word and Universal Plan, so He encoded an indefinite amount of knowledge and wisdom, including complicated science and technological answers. This was genuinely amazing—and it made perfect sense. It's already encoded, but we comprehend more as we advance. Endless levels just keep revealing themselves as we open our minds to the infinite possibilities that fall within the parameters of the love

God created. Leon said, "The secret is to be open-minded enough to allow the unfolding of God's grandeur. We can never put God in a box and say, this is all there is."

I was also struck by his comment that the lack of love creates judgment of others. The minister felt very much at peace when the angels finally got him to understand the true nature of love, forgiveness, and acceptance. He said, "Love is the basic truth of God, and peace will come to us in the end." That is a great comfort for both the dying and the living.

The other insight Leon left was that "the sooner we learn to love and forgive others and ourselves, the easier our transition to next world. Our angels are always present, and eager to lead us toward paradise and protect us along the way, however, most of our judgments and fears block that connection. It is our intense, physical, emotional, social, and spiritual suffering at the end of our lives that allows us to be free from our judgments. It is at this point that our primordial fears come crashing down, allowing us to see what has always been on the other side: unconditional love."

Leon's last piece of loving advice spoke of the importance of tearing down the metaphorical walls that keep us from loving others and ourselves. Working on it "now," instead of tomorrow, assures us of at least twice as much love, peace, and blessings in this world and the next. It is at this point that immeasurable blessings occur.

Chapter 4

The Dreamer

Some of my staff knew Susan earlier in her life. She was a registered nurse, and her case was a long time coming to hospice. At age 39, she had been in a vegetative state for three years, and at the heart of a debate between her family and husband. Her family and friends knew that Susan intended to put a living will into effect to ensure that no heroic measures, including artificial nutrition, would be carried out. This was never to be realized. Without a signed living will, her husband was legally able to make her medical decisions. Her family was overcome with added grief, feeling certain that William, her husband, would pursue an aggressive life-sustaining plan as a means of coping with his guilt. It was obvious to everyone who knew William that his guilt was caused by the events that contributed to her current condition. This was extremely traumatic to Susan's family and close friends, who had to sit back and watch a beautiful woman succumb to the ravages of a vegetative state.

Susan had always been a vibrant, life-affirming, and compassionate woman of service. When I met her kind-hearted parents, they shared their daughter's tragic story with me. She had been raised Christian, but she had a dream early in her life in which a beautiful, white-glowing angel revealed her humanitarian work with the Buddhist citizens of Tibet. She continued to remind her parents of the angelic plan and insisted it was her life path. They were concerned for her safety in the unstable region of Tibet, but Susan was so strong and adamant about her beliefs that they were compelled to support her with her life mission.

She graduated from the University of Texas at Austin with a nursing degree and, while there, she also took a course in theology, including Eastern philosophy, in preparation for her life path. She continued having angelic dreams, which became more centered on her career as a nurse. Eventually, she went to Nepal and Tibet, where she lived for five years. During her tenure there, she met William, a wonderful and spiritual Chinese man who had found his way to that region to help stop the atrocities his country was inflicting on the peaceful people of Tibet. Captivated by their mutual desire to help the Tibetan people as well as their love for the Buddhist faith, they fell in love and married. Within six weeks of their marriage, the Chinese escalated their attacks on the region, and arrested and beheaded many Tibetan sympathizers. Fearing for their lives, William and Susan decided to move back to Houston, where they could start a family and continue their peace efforts for the Tibetans. After arriving in Houston, Susan continued her nursing and spiritual work, and once again found herself guided by the angels. William, without a degree or U.S. citizenship, found it almost impossible to find a job that was fulfilling. This did not bother Susan, but it began to weigh heavily on her husband.

The couple subsequently had three children and, after her first pregnancy, Susan was diagnosed with Type II diabetes. She struggled with oral diabetic medicines, as well as multiple types of insulin regimens, in an unsuccessful attempt to stabilize her blood sugars. She then became, about three years after her diagnosis, the first recipient of the implantable insulin pump. Following the implantation of the device, the doctors noted incredible improvement in her blood sugars. Unfortunately, her husband, who was by this time constantly irritable, was uncomfortable with the disfiguring appearance of the pump on her body, and he told her to have it removed. She refused, and William grew increasingly distressed and argumentative. In a fit of rage, he grabbed the pump under her skin and twisted it. Somehow the pump released a large dose of insulin into Susan's system, which resulted in an immediate drop in her blood sugar to lethal levels. She was immediately rushed to the hospital and shortly thereafter slipped into a hypoglycemic coma.

After being given concentrated doses of dextrose, Susan was rushed to the intensive care unit, where she stabilized. Her eyes were open, and she seemed to be looking at you, but was unable to speak or communicate in any other manner. Minimal brain function was detected on an EEG that was performed 24 hours later. It appeared that her brain had suffered irreversible damage. Without the ability to eat, she had a gastostomy feeding tube placed, and aggressive physical therapy was initiated. Four weeks later, the only improvement was her ability to smile and blink. She was subsequently transferred to a nursing home facility, where she lived for three years. This contradicted her mother's and father's clear understanding of Susan's wishes, as well as the nurses and doctors on staff who knew she wanted "no heroic measures." Because her husband had medical power of attorney, though, they had to follow his guilt-laden wishes. For the next three years, Susan's family and friends fought to place her in hospice and carry out her wish to die naturally. During this time, her husband spent very little time with her, which further alienated the family. Finally, with no apparent reason, William agreed to remove the support and admit her to hospice. When he was asked what changed his mind, he said that he had an epiphany but would not discuss it further.

When I first met William, he acknowledged that he had great guilt over what had happened and said he wanted to make amends. He admitted that his selfish actions had led to Susan's demise. I asked what made him change his mind about bringing her to hospice, and he told me about his vision. His wife had appeared to him with multiple angels that surrounded his bed. He remembers his wife smiling her usual big smile and telling him to let her go. She said, "I have forgiven you. Now you need to forgive yourself, so I can move on. It's time now." The angels never spoke in a voice he could hear, but he sensed their agreement and support of what she was saying. He said that the vision repeated itself over and over that night, and was followed, each time, with an increasing number of angels. "Susan told me that the 50 angels around my bed were not going to leave until I found peace and self-forgiveness. The angels kept changing the way they looked and, at a certain point, they changed to indigo blue with piercing blue eyes and long shiny blonde hair. When I looked up, the spiritual beings were massive. It was obvious to me that this could not just be guilt creating these images. I know my wife, and the angels were actually trying to help me understand my selfish actions. For months, I was actually praying for forgiveness and strength to let Susan go. God, the angels, and Susan heard my prayer. The amount of unconditional love on the other side is simply mind-boggling."

William explained that after what appeared to be months, one of the brightest angels spoke out. "In a kind and gentle voice, he told me that Susan was suffering and she needed my help. I asked, 'How can she be suffering if she is smiling and joyful?' They told me that her suffering transcends our earthly idea of suffering. This will be fully explained during your spiritual release." William said the angel went on to explain that Susan was bound to him as his wife and, as such, she was feeling the same intensity of his guilt, and at times even more. They told him that she had actually accepted most of his guilt over the last several months, so that his peace of mind would lend him the opportunity to rekindle his relationship with their children and to develop new friendships. With these new loving attachments, the earthly bond with Susan could be broken.

William continued: "The tall dark blue angel then sent a light from its chest that penetrated Susan's and mine simultaneously, creating an incredible triangle of blue-white light. At that moment, I began to experience everything that Susan had experienced for the last three years. The angelic apparitions told me it was necessary to feel it completely. This would ultimately give me the strength to let Susan go." Sobbing, he said that the emotional and spiritual pain was so intense that it felt as though he was falling into total darkness. As he fell deeper into the dark abyss, he felt a growing sense of loss and separation from the heavenly realm. Then, in what appeared to be a split second, he found himself awake and questioning what had transpired.

"William, how were you feeling after this experience?" I asked.

"I was shaking and crying and not sure if it had been a dream or a vision. My clothes were torn off my body and the fragrance of Chanel perfume penetrated everything in the room. You know, my wife was wearing that fragrance the night I grabbed the pump." The experience was so overwhelming and real that he immediately called his in-laws and agreed to transfer his wife to hospice and carry out her wishes: to die naturally and in comfort. The family contacted me immediately, and within two hours I had transferred Susan to our facility for evaluation and symptom management.

When I first saw her, I hugged her tightly and told her she was in hospice and that I was going to take away her pain. Almost instantly, she gave me a big smile as tears rolled down her cheeks. I asked her to blink if she was in pain. She blinked repeatedly. When I asked if she was hungry, she did not blink for several seconds. *"Susan, how about the feeding tube? Does it hurt?"* Again, she blinked in a continual fashion. *"Do you want comfort measures, Susan?"* This time she blinked and grimaced over and over, until I reassured her that I understood. Despite the fact that her tests showed she had minimal cognitive function, I was sure it was quite the opposite: She was cognizant enough to understand what she was feeling and had developed a way of communicating. I told her that her husband and family were all coming together now in peace and were going to make sure she was comfortable. What I saw in her eyes at that moment will always be imprinted in my heart and soul. She was definitely a highly evolved spirit.

On further examination, her lungs were clear of fluid, her kidney function was normal, and her vitals were stable. At that point, discontinuing her feedings or fluids would be construed as starvation, and this was a clear violation of my oath as a doctor. I needed a miracle. The next day, the nurse noted on her chart that her urine output had decreased dramatically to only a scant amount and that she had developed pulmonary edema (a large amount of fluid in her lungs). Tests revealed that she was in kidney failure and subsequent fluid overload. That was my sign. This woman had normal kidney function and vital signs for three years and, within 24 hours of coming to hospice, she declined in a way that made it appropriate and necessary to stop further fluids and feeding. It was apparent to me that God was in charge. I said a little prayer of gratitude, and I stopped the feedings and initiated comfort measures. This included morphine for shortness of breath, diuretics to reduce fluid, and sedatives for her extreme anxiety. She immediately went into a deep sleep, and her distress dissipated.

Susan's husband and family spent the last few days of her life working on mending their relationship. During the last two days of Susan's life, I had a vivid dream where, during my examination, her heart stopped and her spirit popped out of her body. She stretched her arms out wide, looked at me with her warm smile, and said, "What a trip." At that instant, I felt an incredible wave of joy and saw her angels dressed in gold, white, and blue light. These entities asked me to convey to

Susan's mother that she would be fine and that her daughter would corroborate this message. Susan then took me by the hand and carried me into the sky high above the earth. Immediately, I was able to see the countless souls leaving their bodies and flying into space, all of them confirming that life was an incredible experience. I also saw a multitude of angels around the earth, guiding the souls and piercing the star-filled canopy and disappearing into space, maybe into another dimension. She told me she had to leave me and that one day, I, too, would accept that my lessons were joyful. She said to never worry and that we're always being taken care of, watched over, no matter what our decisions. We will always have a chance to review our choices and atone for them. I suddenly woke from this awe-inspiring dream, and just stayed in bed for sometime contemplating the messages and being mesmerized by the power of the mind. Later that morning, as I headed back to the hospital, I could not help but wonder how things with Susan would transpire.

When I arrived at the hospital and entered Susan's room, her mother and sister greeted me with warm smiles that looked exactly as Susan's smile in my dream had. After my examination, I was sure that Susan was hours from dying. I reassured her family that she was peaceful, pain-free, not suffocating, and ready to make her final journey. They were both visibly sad but relieved that her suffering was almost over. I believed the timing was right to recount my dream, so I started and, somewhere in the middle, Susan's sister said she had the same dream, and continued where I left off and finished it. I was in shock. She had the same dream and the same messages. Susan's mother was clearly relieved that her prayer was answered. She had prayed for confirmation that her daughter was at peace and able to walk and talk again. She was convinced that Susan had made it to the other side. Within 30 minutes of hugging and sharing, Susan woke up, opened her eyes, smiled, and reached for her husband, who had just arrived. With great effort, she quietly told her husband, mother, and sister she loved them. As she smiled that beautiful smile I had seen in the dream once more, her hand fell gently to the bed, and she was gone. Her family had a great sense of closure and forgiveness that day. I laughed to myself as I remembered her popping out of her body and saying, "What a trip," and floating off into space. Yes, Susan, "what a trip" indeed.

Doctor's Notes and More Dialogue With Susan

Susan's sister, Jan, described some other encounters months before her sister passed. She had seen angels and had been shown that intense healing was occurring between her family and William. On several occasions, Jan saw monks in the room praying for her, while Susan was sitting in a lotus position. Jan would close her eyes, and on reopening, the monks would disappear and her sister would go back to her vegetative state. Jan said she heard the monks helping Susan understand her life lessons. Jan would doubt what she had seen, but Susan told her many stories about these amazing monks in Tibet. She recounted that the same monks appeared at her death and seemed to be guarding her. Jan saw them cover her in gold and maroon cloth, and prayed and chanted the entire time. They prayed for her soul to reach nirvana.

Jan recalls seeing a bright blue light radiate from the top of her head towards the ceiling. Within seconds, the light and the monks were gone. "I am not crazy, Dr. Lerma. I know what I saw. I will never forget it." I explained to Jan that, at their death, monks traditionally encircle the bed, cover the body in a colorful gold and maroon garment, and pray for an average of eight hours that the soul reaches the heavenly realm. The more enlightened one is, the higher in the physical body that the soul is released. The highest is the top of your head. "Dr. Lerma, this information is confirmation that my sister made it to heaven and that she has reached enlightenment. Hmm, it's nice to personally know an enlightened being."

"Yes, Jan, that is comforting."

As for William, he began to atone for his vain and angry action that resulted in Susan's death. He had another dream in which she thanked him for letting her go and repeated her forgiveness. He understands that they had agreed to the circumstances of their lives. He now devotes his time assisting the American Diabetic Association in lobbying insurance companies to provide insulin pumps for diabetics. He is also working with family violence counseling. In my dream, Susan said she knew her husband would atone and negotiated to stay until he was ready. Married now, William's new wife has developed breast cancer, and he has made a commitment to stay with her, and to be supportive and fully present. He feels it is a lesson to further his understanding of compassion and service. William continues to speak about angels and their teachings of self-love, self-forgiveness, and total love. He is a powerful speaker with an amazing story, and, as the angels have repeatedly told many of my patients, one person can change the whole world.

Chapter 5

Angel Feathers

I had just sat down and ordered lunch at one of my favorite restaurants when my pager went off: Our new patient had just arrived. I grabbed my food and ate on the run again.

Katarina, a 42-year-old Hispanic woman with two daughters, ages 14 and 16, was in the final stages of cervical cancer. This type of malignancy is always difficult to witness, because most, if not all, cases could have been prevented with regular gynecological care. Even more difficult to understand are the reasons women give for not seeking gynecological care, including a lack of education, shyness, socioeconomic status, and poor access to medical care. To die these days from a potentially curable disease is beyond comprehension.

The cases are often identical: young women in the prime of their lives, often beautiful, but their bodies swollen and full of fluid from undiagnosed and untreated cancers. Their bodies have turned into their enemies. It's a slow and painful process, and, because it usually does not involve the brain, patients are intensely aware of everything that happens.

This case seemed particularly sad to me. Katarina was a former lounge singer with a history of drug use and high-risk behaviors stemming from sexual abuse early in her life. However, just two years earlier, with her life going nowhere and her daughters begging her to change, she decided to give herself back to God. As the lead vocalist in a prominent evangelical choir, Katarina's beautiful voice and songs inspired many to return to God. She witnessed trials and tribulations around her and devoted the majority of her time to helping others who were still in the midst of their addictions and abuses. During this time, the biggest trial of her life was about to present itself in the form of terminal cancer.

When I met her for the first time, I was struck by her ethereal beauty and the way she was trying so hard to maintain her dignity. She was dressed in a lovely gown and wearing makeup, and her long shiny black hair was brushed back and neatly braided. But she couldn't hide her distended abdomen and hugely swollen legs, her skin stretched so tight it leaked fluid constantly. Her mother and daughters were with her, looking frightened, aware that the transfer to the inpatient hospice unit meant that Katarina was close to death. Her mom, Maria, and dad, Joseph, were very spiritual and devout Catholics from Monterrey, Mexico, with a strong marriage of more than 50 years. Her brothers and sisters were equally spiritual and had not followed the same hard road Katarina had chosen.

The day we admitted her, Katarina was alert but bed-bound, and we spent a great deal of time talking. I wanted to make her feel comfortable in every way possible, medically and emotionally. Our connection grew rapidly, and she began sharing her fears of dying and her regrets in life. With her voice quivering, she asked only one question: "Dr. Lerma, how long do I have to live?" I told her that, because the fluid in her lungs was worsening and because she had not been able to eat in four or five days as a result of her intestinal obstruction, her short-term prognosis was grim, about seven to 10 days. She cried inconsolably and said she was not ready to die. She clung to me, and I spent most of the afternoon comforting and reassuring her and her mom. Her daughters could not handle the intense emotions, so I had the social worker provide counseling. Recalling my own reaction to my father's terminal illness, I was able to empathize and understand Katarina's and her family's pain.

To lighten the mood, I told her some of my patients' angelic stories and asked her if she had seen any angels yet. That triggered something in her that initiated the recounting of her life story. I listened and empathized with her and the seeming injustice of it all, especially after she had made such great changes in her life.

A few months prior to her diagnosis, Katarina had moved to Houston and was working "singing for God," as she called it. At that time, she began to experience severe lower abdominal pains, and eventually she went to an emergency room to be examined. With her limited English, no insurance, and her history of drug use, doctors quickly labeled her a drug-seeker and discharged her with a simple diagnosis of pre-menstrual pain. A few weeks later, she started bleeding vaginally, and repeated visits to the emergency room resulted in a diagnosis of dysmenorrheal. Upon discharge, she was told to use Tylenol for her pain. Feeling desperate and abandoned, and in excruciating pain, she resorted to using street morphine or heroin for her pain. Katarina felt she had no other choice, because the medical community did not help her. She was being drawn back into her old life, but she fought it desperately because she did not want to fail God and her family. As the pain worsened, so did her use of street opiates. With her pain better controlled with the morphine and heroin, Katarina felt that she was improving. However, this couldn't be further from the truth, as her cancer was now beyond cure.

Katarina told me about a dream she had only days before her diagnosis, where the Archangel Gabriel boldly stated, "You have been chosen. The events in your life are transpiring in perfection and will ultimately help many souls find there way back to God." She understood that this message was not the drugs or disease speaking and, without further words, she accepted this calling that would help her, her family, and the world. The Archangel Michael unfolded the entire plan and reassured her that God and the angels would be with her and were going to allow her diagnosis to be made so she could have adequate comfort from her pain. Two days later, with her pain and bleeding escalating, she went to another emergency room. After reviewing her medical records, the doctors once again thought she was drug-seeking and refused to treat her. Crying as she left the emergency room, she ran into a physician who stopped to find out what was wrong. Noticing her broken English, he spoke to her in Spanish, asking her, "¿Que pasa, senorita?"("What's wrong, miss?") With those words of compassion, Katrina hugged him and said, "Ayuda me. Ayuda me, por favor." ("Help me. Help me, please.")

She was unaware that she was talking with a doctor, an obstetrician and gynecologist on staff at the hospital. She told him she was bleeding and that the emergency doctors didn't want to do anything for her. Perhaps inspired by her angel or perhaps just feeling empathetic that evening, he took pity on her and walked her back to the hospital, where he found that she was extremely anemic. He admitted Katarina to the gynecology floor where he ordered blood work and a CT scan of her abdomen and pelvis. The results prompted a biopsy of her cervix. The frozen sections and results from her tumor markers and scans revealed advanced cervical cancer with metastasis throughout her abdomen and lungs with obstruction of the lymph system to her lower extremities. An oncologist immediately evaluated Katarina, and began chemotherapy and radiation treatments as well as pain control. It was just as the angel had said: She got help with the pain, but was left with a terminal diagnosis.

At the start of her chemotherapy, her angel Michael appeared and explained that he was sending a different angel every night to comfort her and remind her that she would not be abandoned by God. That evening, a large translucent, white-robed angel appeared, and just stood to the right of her bed in a shielding and comforting stance. A different angel appeared every night thereafter to comfort her, and always in the same place. She was unclear why they chose to appear to her right, but she felt it was protective in nature. Curious, I asked her to describe the angels' appearances. She said, "Their faces were brilliant and their long blonde to brown silky hair blended with their feathers and long-flowing robes." The angels stayed for about five to 10 minutes every night to console her, yet she would cry and beg it not to depart. It was at those times of despair that she felt abandoned by God. She kept asking, "How could God do this after I gave my life back to Him? I'm so angry at Him!"

One of the angels told her it was fine to act that way and to feel what she was feeling, as this showed God that she loved and acknowledged Him; all God really wants is for us to acknowledge and have a relationship with Him. The angel commented that God fully understands our pain, suffering, and despair as well as the difficulty of their purpose, because He lives within us and experiences it with us. In addition to being consoled, Katarina was told that the miracle of life and its answers were within her reach.

Within the first day of her admission into hospice, Katarina's agonizing pain was under control. This gave her the needed peace to begin the process of closure. Per Katarina's request, her family gathered together to discuss her wishes before dying. With her parents and sisters present around her bed, I asked Katarina who she wanted to care for her children. She said the angel told her that her sister Maria had the time and spiritual desire to foster their mission in life. Katarina knew this was the right choice, because her children had always been drawn to Maria's motherly love. At that moment, Maria told Katarina that she would see it as an honor to care for them—especially after a recent dream she had in which seven beautiful white-glowing angels expressed the same desire. Katarina was elated that her vision was confirmed. Her most weighing concern was lifted, and Katarina was enveloped by total tranquility.

Katarina continued to describe the angel's prophetic visions. She said the next vision was projected on the forward wall of the room, as if it were a motion picture. She saw her daughters growing up to help other people and carrying on an incredible legacy for the family of healing through music and through witnessing. Katarina was also able to see herself communing with

Jesus and agreeing to her life's direction. She saw that what she had agreed to was much greater than the suffering she would experience. Katarina smiled, and said she was able to remember that conversation and finally understood the significance of her life in relation to God's plan. She said that we will all be reminded of our choices to help fulfill God's plan. She now discussed suffering as the angels revealed to her: "We all suffer in some form or fashion, and our suffering is part of nature, but joy is also present, and that is what suffering builds into itself: joy."

She had a sense that what she was doing was not just for her family or herself but for the whole world. Completely filled with sorrow, everyone in her room began to weep. Katarina's mother was crying, but was joyful, and was able to release her daughter to God. Katarina also accepted her death, and this was incredible, as she had persistently denied that she was dying even while having visions of magnificent spiritual beings. I asked her what truly changed her mind, and she replied that it was simply knowing that her children would be loved and cared for by her sister the same as she would care for them.

Four days before her death, at around one in the morning, Katarina woke her mother and whispered that a new magnificent angel, large and brilliantly blue with white wings, had appeared. Her mother said, "I saw my daughter focus on the right side of her bed, smiling and lifting her hands up as she began a voiceless conversation into space. I could see her mouth moving but I could hear no sound, and her head and eyes were shifting back and forth as though she was watching a moving object." Her mom kept observing her and trying to read her lips. Suddenly, it was as if the volume was turned up and she could hear her daughter's voice. She heard her say, in Spanish, "Okay, just give me something to let me know you're coming back." Then, Katarina nodded, reached up, clasped her hand into a fist, and brought it to her bosom and smiled, "Thank you. Thank you."

Her mom heard that, but was not sure what was transpiring. Katarina said, "Mom, do you want to look at what I have? What the angel gave me?"

Her mother said, "Of course, my love. What do you have?"

Katarina said softly, "The angel was here, and I grabbed one of his feathers." She slowly opened her palm, and there was a perfectly shaped white, fluffy feather in her hand, about 6 inches long. She knew I would be excited about this, so she eagerly waited to show me the feather. Her mother put the feather in a plastic bag, and Katarina told her to give it to me in gratitude for the loving care I provided to her family and her. I didn't feel I could accept such a gift, but I also did not want to offend her. At that moment I was paged to see a new patient, so I left, telling her we could discuss it another day. A couple of days later, Katarina pleaded that I take the feather as a gift from her and God. How could I refuse? I told her I would always cherish it and hoped that its story would help comfort my other patients. Katarina smiled and said that was a wonderful plan.

When her mother removed the little plastic bag with the feather safely protected in it, she was shocked to find that it had shrunk to less than 1 inch, about the size of a pillow feather. Interestingly, most if not all acute-care facilities, including our facility, had strict regulations in place that prevented the use of feather pillows, due in part to the high incidence of allergic reactions. Most, if not all, pillows are filled with varying types of foam and securely covered with a soft plastic material. I checked all the pillows in Katarina's room, and all were soft foam, and her mother denied bringing any pillows from home. We were all stunned. Her mother said, "Dr. Lerma, you saw the feather two days ago and was it not close to 6 inches?"

"*Absolutely,*" I responded.

Katarina's mother continued, "Well, I think this feather is shrinking. Do you think it's meant to disappear? Please, Dr. Lerma, keep it and let me know if it does. People will believe it if you tell them the story. You're a doctor, after all." I agreed and, with the feather still in the bag, I locked it in my desk drawer.

When I shared the story with a nurse at our facility, she recounted a similar story she heard from our janitor, Jeffrey, earlier that day. I called him and asked him to repeat the story he had told the nurse. He began, "Dr. Lerma, remember Mr. Willie, the nice man across the hall from Katarina? Just the other day, while I was cleaning his room, I heard the patient talking in his sleep and saying that an angel had given him a feather to remind him that the angels are always with him. I noticed a large feather lying on the floor. I was amazed, and I wondered if this feather was truly an angel feather. It was quite beautiful, white and pretty large. It must have been around 8 to 10 inches. I know feathered pillows are not allowed in our hospice, and thought it was from his home pillow or someone brought it to him. Well, he had no family members or personal pillows. So I picked it up and put it on the bedside table under the edge of a flower vase so it wouldn't blow away. The next day, I noticed that it looked considerably smaller, but I was not sure. Then, today the patient died, and, when I went to clean the room, I noticed the feather was gone.

"That is when I spoke with his nurse and asked if she had seen it or thrown it away. She said she remembers seeing it yesterday, but today it was gone. Dr. Lerma, I'm not sure what happened to it, but I had my suspicions. It was meant to disappear." I could not believe the similarities. Maybe Katarina's mother was right when she said that the feather might disappear. I quickly went to see if Katarina's feather was in my desk drawer, and, sure enough, it was there and was still the same size as when I received it.

The next day Katarina died peacefully with her children, sisters, and mother present. They were clearly sad, but filled with the angelic experiences that gave them total peace. Wondering if her feather had disappeared as Mr. Willie's had, I went to my office to check on the feather. When I unlocked the drawer and removed the bag, I immediately noticed the feather was not in the bag. I looked all around and could not find it. The feather had indeed disappeared. I was the only one with a key to my desk, and I had told no one I had placed it there. At that moment I recalled that Katarina had asked for it and needed it as a reminder that the angel would return to take her to heaven. She no longer needed the feather as a reminder: She was on the white, feathered wings of her angel at last. The feather had served its purpose and had now become entwined with faith. I smiled, wondering if anyone would ever believe such a fantastic tale. All that truly mattered was that Katarina finally knew the universal truth.

Doctor's Notes
and More Dialogue With Katarina

Katarina's mother and daughters were greatly comforted by the feather in the days prior to her death. It was a symbol that some how confirmed for them that Katarina had truly changed her life and was truly helping others. Katarina had finally come to that realization, too, and perhaps that's why her family could finally accept it. Katarina and I had many conversations about what the angels were teaching her.

The angels told Katarina not to feel guilty for the things she saw as mistakes. There are no mistakes. She chose her life path and understood that it was for a greater purpose. Close to the end of her life, the angels brought her visions to comfort and teach her. They showed her the greater purpose in her suffering—not just during her illness, but throughout her life. They explained how the life she had led gave her great compassion and understanding for others with addictions and weaknesses. She came to accept that her addictions were part of her lessons, which led to self-forgiveness, self-love, and peace.

She understood that, when God gives us big challenges, He also gives us gifts to comfort us. She had been given her singing voice, which brought great comfort and hope to many others who had experienced similar lives with addictions and illnesses. About her music, she said, "The singing talent was a gift from God and was something no one could ever take away from me. I was writing incredible songs about God and, because of my gift, many people returned to their faith. I realized that I never left God even when I was at my lowest point. I needed to go through my challenges so I could teach myself, and ultimately others, that they can do it too. I was told by the angels that I am an older soul, and I chose to come here and lead others to their missions. I was shown how my kids will also be part of the music ministry. They have a mission that my life has contributed to." She understood her life in a completely different way, and she accepted it all.

She said the angels also met her in her reality and showed her beautiful things that brought her joy and comfort. They sang her favorite songs and invited her to sing with them. Sometimes she would be lying in the bed singing in angelic tones, which sent out a peace that was palpable to everyone present.

Katarina loved the beach and water in general, and the angels understood that this was familiar to her, so they let her swim in her favorite beaches and bask in the sun to give her reprieve from pain. She said, "These dream-like, but vivid experiences create an overwhelming sense of peace that engulfs your essence." The angels also allowed her to continue experiencing her children's love and be involved in their emotional and spiritual growth.

I asked her, *"How do we finally let go of our most precious loved ones?"*

"The angels show us just enough of heaven—our true home, if you will—to remind us that in this place all is possible, with Christ's love. There is unimaginable joy and we are drawn to it. It is through joy that we can create changes in our lives and in our world. And help those loved ones back on earth."

"Why is heaven so familiar to us?"

"Because, as the Bible says, when we accept God we also accept His kingdom/heaven to penetrate every fiber of our being. God understands our individual perceptions of heaven and reflects them back to us, and this results in comfort, peace, joy, and unconditional love. When we are joyous, that is heaven. Here on earth."

Katarina spoke of the chance God gives us all on our death-bed to bring about generational healing. For her, she was able to heal unresolved issues that she and her grandparents had before they died. Without this healing, neither party can move forward to experience God's total forgiveness and love. It is vital to clear up as many issues here on earth before being called to our home with God.

Katarina finally let go of all the suffering and doubt, and, even though her body was experiencing it, her spirit was not as she was, often detached from her body. Roughly three to five days before anyone dies, angels and deceased loved ones are present almost 24 hours a day. During this time angels are aiding family members in obtaining their closure. Most often, the patient has already had his or her life review and has negoti-ated, through unconditional love, to stay in his or her body until family and friends attain peace. The sooner the family mem-bers release their fears, pathological attachments to the dying, anger, hatred, and so forth, the sooner their loved one will pass to the heavenly realm.

Most patients who linger for weeks are often being kept on the earthly plane due to someone else's selfish reasons or, rarely, a patient's own deep-rooted and unresolved darkness. This latter issue is very difficult to watch, and is an issue that will be carried on to the next world. Prayer for these patients is most effective.

The bottom line is that it is all about our free will. Katarina emphasized that I tell everyone to not wait to work your issues on your deathbed. This is too overwhelming. The key is now—today. Develop true understanding of who you are—your weaknesses and your strengths. Then just love yourself, for you were made perfect. Most people in the world do not love themselves because they always want to be someone else. This is the root of all evil. If one cannot love oneself, then how can he or she love others? That is why the divorce rate in the United States is greater than 60 percent. There is no true love for the spouse. Bigotry, hatred, discrimination, racial profiling, religious wars, fear—all of these are a result of the non-existent self-love.

The angels told Katarina there are very holy people on earth that are born specifically to be examples of this love. Gandhi, Pope John Paul II, Mother Theresa, the Dalai Lama, and even some of our parents that have been married for years are examples of true self-lovers. One does not need to get it perfect. All one has to do is stay balanced. Stay away from both extremes, as this is a recipe for sure failure. Being too religious creates, ironically, fear and judgment. We all have a dark side and a light side. Attempt to achieve balance and strive to become as fluid as Christ with regard to the entire continuum of experiences. He would help people on both ends of the social spectrum, from prostitutes to religious leaders, including Pharisees.

This takes a lot of work; the angels said it can be done, but only with the help of God. So, Katarina said, love yourself and forgive yourself, then try to love and forgive others. One will see that it will get easier. Christ died for us because He knew we were going to continually sin, and this gave us infinite number of chances to at least understand the concept. Remember, though, Katarina said, one never knows the time God will call us to leave this world. Just try and be kind to oneself and others and believe in the Lord Jesus Christ as your savior. "You won't be disappointed," Katarina said.

I asked her about her life review and she said, "John, you wouldn't understand it. You will only understand your own. There is no language for it. Even if I tried to tell you, I couldn't express it. It's all spoken in feelings." I started asking some basic questions, but she didn't like that. She preferred to tell me things as she felt them. She said that every patient has an angel, or many angels, and that they will all see their deceased loved ones. They will all understand their purpose and their life choices before they go.

What Katarina said next was somewhat challenging to my belief systems, but something resonated within me, so I thought it important to share it. She said, "We choose our lives, but we don't remember that choice. When the angels show our life to us, they give back the memory of that choice, and then we know our truth. Nothing is forced on us. We are all working together. We're part of the consciousness of the whole world. We're growing as a group. If some of us get sick, every human being is emotionally affected, even if they don't realize it. For instance, when some of us choose the dark side, others have to take on the incredible energy of that darkness and defeat it so as to restore balance. It can come to you in many ways, emotionally, spiritually, and sometimes through physical illness. I was shown that even the cancer cells are still of God. By choosing to take on another person's darkness, I accelerated my cell growth so fast that I got cancer."

I asked her, *"Did you get to see the positive effects that resulted from your cancer and your suffering?"*

She said, "Yes," and it mainly affected the direction of her children's path.

The bereavement team followed Katarina's family for about one year and was able to see how the family was growing and coping. Her daughters were living with Maria and her husband, as had been decided. They attend church, sing with the choir, and give testimony about their mom, and great emotional healing has occurred for the family, as well as for others who hear Katarina's story. They help people understand that, no matter what extremes they have gone to in their lives, there is always a way back to God and to their center. Katarina's message of unconditional love had indeed affected her family and others, as she had hoped.

For me, I now understand that everything has its purpose. Through my work at hospice, I have given up judging the choices others make. We are all really the same, no matter how good or bad we think we are. Once again, the lessons learned from those who are exiting this life are profound, and I have to keep expanding as I am presented with new information. I am humbled and gratified to be exposed to such wisdom, and I never lack for new things to ponder and wonder about. I am glad I chose this path, and I am glad I now understand and know that I made that choice with God's direction.

Chapter 6

Deep Remorse

William came from Argentina for treatment for his lung cancer at the world-renowned MD Anderson Cancer Institute in Houston, Texas. After three months of intensive treatment, he was transferred to our hospice facility, as even the experimental protocols failed to stop the spread of his aggressive malignancy. Shortly after his admission, his level of cognitive function rapidly declined, leaving him almost comatose and intermittently delirious. During this time, he frequently flailed around on the bed and often spoke in German, screaming for help, and saying, "Heil Hitler" and other German army salutations. I wiped the sweat from his brow and touched his arms soothingly. I found it strange that he spoke German, but his wife confirmed that they were both born and raised in Berlin, Germany, and fled to Argentina shortly after the beginning of World War II.

When we treated the cause of his delirium, which was dehydration, his level of consciousness improved. He began to communicate and asked a multitude of questions, including, "Where am I? Am I dead? Was I talking about the War?" I told him that he was alive and in hospice because his cancer was no longer treatable. "What about World War II and Hitler? Did I speak of that time, and was my family present during these times?"

I told him, *"Yes. In fact you were speaking German and saying, 'Heil Hitler.' No, your family was not in the room during that time."*

He instantly started crying and begged me not to tell anyone what I heard him say, especially his family. I reassured William I would keep his secrets and would never judge anything he ever did or said. I reminded him I was solely there to relieve his physical, emotional, spiritual, and interpersonal pain, and that, if at any time he wanted to discus his life's concerns, I was there to listen.

Over the next week, William and I developed a trusting relationship, and one morning William chose to disclose that he had been an officer in the SS, Hitler's army, during World War II, and he had directly witnessed and participated in the extermination of his race. He wept as he told me this, and he seemed truly remorseful. He described how he locked Christians and Jews, both young and old, in the showers and turned his back while other trained soldiers pumped cyanide gas through the showerheads. He recalled one night when a beautiful Jewish woman stopped before entering the showers and looked him straight in the eyes. There was no fear in her face, and the look of true compassion burned into his soul. This vision haunted him for the rest of his life.

William's command of this concentration camp was short-lived, as he developed a sudden and life-threatening pulmonary disease. He poisoned himself with a small amount of cyanide, hoping this would make him ill enough to keep him permanently out of the war and away from the atrocities. Never knowing his plan, Hitler's physicians attributed his grave illness to secondary exposure of cyanide gas. Instead of being court-martialed for attempted suicide, he was awarded one of the highest awards for bravery and service to his homeland. With his lungs permanently damaged, William never returned to his command.

When I asked him why he joined the SS, he said his work in biochemistry caught the attention of Hitler's elite army, and he was asked to help his country attain freedom from the tyrannical leaders of the world. He respectfully refused, and within hours several SS soldiers arrested his wife and children. The Nazis had records of all Jews in Germany and discovered that William, a full-blooded German, had married a Jewish woman, and so his children were part Jewish. They made it clear that all Jews were to be arrested for their acts of tyranny against Hitler's Third Reich and be sentenced to death. William explained, "I had to save my family. I could not let them die the way millions of others I heard were dying. How human beings could put me in a place where I had to choose between saving my family or saving someone else's family— this is how Hitler got people to follow his horrific orders. Everyone was choosing to save their families, and close off their heart and morals. In just hours, we transformed from God-loving family men to cold-hearted killers. All I could think of was how much evil I had to commit to do good." William was so lifeless as he recalled the most horrible event this world had ever witnessed.

Given no alternative, he agreed to join the SS, contingent on allowing his family to leave Germany. The Nazi officials agreed, and freed his family in exchange for his aid in furthering research in biological warfare. As the war escalated, so did Hitler's call to improve efficiency in extermination. William, along with other colleagues, was reassigned to concentration camps, where multiple biological and genetic experiments were being conducted. Here he finally saw the scope of Hitler's evil plan and realized the mistake he had made in deciding to save his family.

Other than the use of cyanide gas for extermination of Jews and Christians, William would not discuss research that he had witnessed. I did not press him, but I could not help but wonder if it was something worse than genocide. "Dr. Lerma, I made a deal with the devil and I can't take it back. It's too late for me. There is no way I will ever see God! I know now what God meant when He said that those who save their lives will lose, and those who lose their lives will have everlasting life." He asked me to forgive him, and I told him there was nothing to forgive and that he had not hurt me. He said, "Oh, but I have. The angels told me that the whole world was devastated by those horrible events, and that everyone who was born after the Holocaust was affected."

"Okay, William. I forgive you," I replied.

He smiled and thanked me. He asked me not to let his children know that he had done these things. "Not even my wife knew the extent of my involvement. I have borne my shame and guilt in silence until now." I felt deep remorse, as he was finally able to unburden his soul to me.

He asked me how long he had been comatose, and I told him it had been about 48 hours. He looked shocked and said, "That's impossible. I know I was in hell for hundreds of years. I just know it." I assured him it had only been two days and asked what he had experienced.

"I was in a dark cave, shoulder to shoulder with many other Nazi and Roman soldiers who had been involved in mass killings. I could hear their thoughts and feel their anguish, and it mirrored my own guilt and shame. The emotional pain was deep and raw, and it was unending and seemed eternal. This was hell, Dr. Lerma."

"William, how did you finally get out?"

"You see, Dr. Lerma, there was always a bright light in the distance, and I felt drawn to it, but I was afraid, not knowing what kind of judgment awaited me. I knew it was the light of God and did not feel worthy to even be seeing it. After what seemed to be years of looking into the light, I finally had enough energy to cry out for help. At once, I noticed the formation of an opening in the distant part of the lifeless cavern. From the small opening, I saw light beings walking past the entrance, back and forth, but never uttering a single word or sound. I assumed they were the guards that kept all of them from leaving, and I cowered from them, ashamed of who I had been.

"As I intensely stared at the light beings, I was finally able to obtain eye contact with the female apparition, and astonishingly, there was something familiar about her clear, blue eyes. They were similar to the eyes of that beautiful Jewish woman I escorted into the cyanide showers. I screamed out to her, 'I'm sorry. I'm so sorry.'" William said that she stopped and turned her head to look into the cave. Feeling ashamed, he stepped back into the darkness and, as she stepped into the darkness, bright white light replaced it. William's soul was now exposed, but the angel's compassion and unconditional love clothed him. He explained, "She spoke in a voice that radiated love to me, 'I forgave you even before you killed me.' She started to walk away again, but I called out, 'Wait, don't go.' She stopped, turned to face me, and extended her arms toward me. 'Come with me and I'll help free you from your guilt.' I hesitated, as I felt that I deserved all the guilt. Yet, there was something so compelling about her that I slowly moved towards her loving arms.

"As I stepped out of the cave, I was bathed in a light that filled me with intense love and joy. The energy was so intense that I started to faint. Falling slowly, I saw her fly towards me and catch me with her soft, feathered wings. Comfortable now, I began to converse about my life. Expressing my sorrow for everything I had done, I told her I attempted to make amends, but nothing would take the coldness from my heart. She said, 'You have a choice. You can accept that you lived the life you chose to live, and forgive yourself and move on. Or, you can experience the pain you caused in order to be released.'" William, looking sad, told her it should not be so easy to be forgiven. "I told her, 'I caused great suffering, and I need to know that suffering in order to release it.' She shook her head sadly and said, 'So be it.'"

In a split second, William said he entered the minds and bodies of every single Jew and Christian he killed at the Nazi concentration camp. He felt their pain, fear, and death all at the same time. He described being in a concentration camp and being killed in a cyanide shower—and at the same time he was in his own body, turning his back on the showers and walking away. He was screaming for mercy and help even as he was ignoring the screams behind him. The people, which he had become, were crying out to him, and asking why and begging him not to do it. He remembered how he wanted to help them, but he was so afraid for his family that he just couldn't do it. The conflict within him was as painful as the deaths of those he killed. Feeling the pain of thousands of adults and children simultaneously was pure horror, William described.

At some point, the woman of light returned and asked William if he was ready to forgive himself, and he said that he was. At that point, all the people he had killed surrounded him, forgave him, and let him know how happy they were that he had been redeemed. She wrapped him in her arms of light and carried him into the greater light of God. He was bathed in unconditional love; it permeated his entire being, and a message filled his cells with the understanding that God had allowed everything that had happened in order to teach humanity to stand up against evil. He was told that, because of free will, man was destined to experience darkness and goodness. God's plan for the independent soul was to learn to evolve away from hatred, fear, arrogance, and pride, and move towards pure love. The Holocaust was not created by God, but rather by the raw darkness within man and intensified by man. It is up to man, with the acknowledgment of God, to not fear or try to control these events, but to learn that, with only God within us, we can defeat that darkness. We cannot do it by ourselves. William said that is the biggest lesson: Learn to depend on God, and He will use your free will to make the right decisions and save humanity.

William revealed to man that we are doomed without God making our decisions. Ultimately, he had agreed to his role as a murderer to help teach this lesson to mankind. The lessons of love and compassion were huge, and hopefully humanity will never again allow this kind of atrocity. All of humanity suffered and grew from the pain of those choices—and all of heaven rejoiced when the lesson was learned and a covenant was made between God and mankind to never allow this again. When a great drama is played out on the earth stage, the whole universe is watching, waiting, and feeling and integrating the lessons. Someone has to play the villains. But now that phase is over; learning through suffering is an old paradigm. It is time to embrace our joy and creativity, and to stop playing the old games and the old roles. It is time to forgive ourselves and let it go, just as William had to do. It is time to embrace our divinity and change our purpose from survival to co-creating a better world. The choice is ours. The time is now, William explained.

During this experience, William finally came to an understanding that the soul lasts forever and that the body is not that important. He really didn't understand that until he was dying. There was no right or wrong in the choices he made. Someone had to die: either his family or the Jewish people. Even if he had allowed his family to die and had given up his own life, the lesson would have continued. He could not have stopped it; it was bigger than he was. However, now that that lesson has been taught, the whole universe has the opportunity to choose love and compassion, and to give aid to those in distress. William realized that they were all one and what he did to others he did to himself. After telling me his amazing story over a two-day period, his children arrived from Argentina, and he died peacefully, leaving me to contemplate man's inhumanity to man and to release my own judgments about other people's choices.

Doctor's Notes and More Dialogue With William

I learned more about the Holocaust and the war than I ever wanted to know. William said that, when the war started, the Germans wanted to take his wife because she looked Jewish. The Germans kept incredible records, he said, and those records included racial profiling. During the war, the Nazis required a physical of most people. The physical examination consisted of body measurements: nasal length, head circumference, distance from eye to eye, height, weight, and chest, waist, and genital proportions. German physicians were given a chart of measurements for Jews, Russians, French, and so forth, and they were to determine which race people belonged to. Under Hitler's reign, scientists said that the Aryan race had a perfected body proportions and that other races were less than perfect. These physical exams enabled the Third Reich to locate Jews and exterminate them. The irony was that Hitler was allegedly part Jewish. Historians believe he had records of his birthplace destroyed to prevent the truth about his past from being revealed.

William said that he chose Argentina after the war and was able to get his family out with some money they had saved. He said that the American government had offered him a job in the area of biogenetics, but he refused, as he had learned that many of the German scientists and engineers that received amnesty in America were forced to live in bunkers in the desert and continue military research. It was apparently not much different than the Nazi regime. He was content to move to Argentina and started a pecan farm.

Over the years, William prospered and became a noted philanthropist. He continued to live in fear that he would be recognized and prosecuted for his crimes, though. He spent his whole life atoning for his past and was never able to exorcise the guilt until the angelic woman brought him understanding and wisdom.

William warned me that the United States had employed many of the scientists who did cloning studies under Hitler experiments, and that they were free to continue their work. He said there is potential danger in that line of research and that it will be our next life lesson. It will be possible to clone any entity with DNA. In the wrong hands, this technology can be used to clone the worst of creations, including Hitler.

I found it very interesting that the angelic woman told William that no angels or other beings can talk to you unless you ask them to. Then I remembered how many of my patients describe that the spiritual beings in the beginning do not speak. They merely smile and appear to be in a protective stance. William explained that free will is respected by spiritual entities. They usually wait for us to invite them into our life for assistance. They can hear our thoughts and will respond to us wondering who they are and what they want. Communication is mainly through extrasensory perception. There are no vocal cords in the spiritual world—just thought.

I asked William about heaven, and he said his experience of it reminded him of a beautiful, perfect Austria. I asked if he saw Jesus, Buddha, or Muhammad there. He said that they are all there, but you don't call them by those names. They're just light beings, expressions of God's energy. No one goes by earth names there. There are hierarchies in heaven with angels who are physically bigger and brighter, and there are angels completely opposite of that. Yet no one is more important than another. I asked about hell, and he asked, "Didn't you hear my story?" He said that what he had been through was hell on earth and that was enough for him. I tend to agree with that.

Chapter 7

The Angelic Nurse

At seven in the morning, the medical residents, the nurses, and I started our daily teaching rounds. In the first room was an 82-year-old woman named Mildred, who was diagnosed with ovarian cancer, widespread metastasis to the bones and lungs, and multiple viscera. She had been in and out of consciousness, and in severe pain the night before. Now that her pain was under control and she was well hydrated, she was astonishingly vibrant and alert. She welcomed the entire medical team into her room and immediately thanked us for taking her pain away.

Mildred explained how excruciating pain caused her to hallucinate, and wax and wane in delirium. "I can barely remember what I experienced, but one thing I do remember, which was a nightmare, was my 10 brothers and sisters crammed into a Volkswagen, traveling across the universe. I certainly hope that was a hallucination," she said, laughing as she recalled her delusion. She allowed us to examine her, and the students obtained further social history from this delightful lady. Before I left the hospital that evening, I checked in on Mildred, who was still pulsating with joy.

"*How are you Mrs. Mildred?*" I asked.

"Dr. Lerma, I've never felt better. I just can't believe my turnaround. I am waiting for my evening sitter, but, before she arrives, I'd like to ask you to explain something."

"*Of course. How can I help you?*"

Mildred went on to explain that, after the medical team walked out of her room in the morning, several people remained. At first she thought they were medical students, but they did not speak, and their lab coats were unusually long and bright white. Within seconds, they disappeared. Being her jovial self, Mildred said, "It must have been those margaritas I had last night."

I laughed and told her not to worry: "*It probably was the medicine you received last night.*"

"Maybe you're right, but why am I am able to see my deceased mother and father as well as those white people next to you, which I think are angels now?" Sensing a sudden chill, I must have looked dumbfounded, because she said, "It's okay, Dr. Lerma. I'm not crazy, and they are very peaceful."

"*Are you sure, Mildred?*"

"Sure as the cancer in my stomach." Not knowing what to say, I simply asked her how she knew they were angels. She said, "I could just tell by the white light that was coming from their entire body. The light is so bright and it makes you feel loved and that everything is going to be okay."

"*Are you seeing your brothers and sisters in that Volkswagen?*" I asked.

"Nope, not since last night."

"Are you feeling sick like last night, or are you anxious or in pain? Did you get any recent sedatives?"

"No to all your questions, Dr. Lerma. The last medicines I received were more than 12 hours ago. Like I said, I have never felt better."

Interested about how these experiences differed from her classic hallucinations from last night, I asked her to elaborate further. "Dr. Lerma, they are no longer here with us, but I swear they were as real as you are."

"Can you tell me what they wanted and what they looked like?"

Mildred went on to say that her parents told her that her angel was coming later that evening to help her cross over to be with them. She described them to be in their early 30s, healthy, and wearing their own regular clothes, although they had been much older when they died. They also told her that her prayer was answered: She was going to be allowed to live long enough to see her family, who were out of the country. They reassured her that all the people and angels she saw were there to support her and protect her from further pain. As her sitter entered the room, Mildred changed the conversation and said she was ready to sleep. I hugged her and told her I would be back at the usual time in the morning to visit with her. She smiled, gave me a kiss on my forehead, and said, "Sleep with the angels, Dr. Lerma."

As Mildred progressed toward her final exit, I had daily visits with her. She continued to describe lights, angelic beings, and family appearances. On the third day, when I walked in, her sitter was already there. I touched Mildred's hands and arms, and she was less responsive but lying peacefully on her bed, with her beautiful white hair spread out on the pillow. Noticing that she was smiling and looking at the corner of the room, I asked her, *"Princess, are you seeing angels again?"* (Mildred loved it when I called her "princess" or "my love." She said it made her feel young again.)

She responded, "Yes. The angels are unusually bright tonight."

"Are they talking to you?"

"No, Dr. Lerma. They're just sending peace my way, and it feels so good." I asked her how many were present. She said, "Right now there is only one in the corner, but sometimes there are between three and 10—all looking different. It's hard to say how big they are, because, when you're looking up towards the corner of the ceiling, it's about 9 feet tall, and somehow they look bigger than that." She seemed to be looking at different corners of the room. She told me, "Behind the angels are majestic mountains and vast forests with animals, birds, and children playing in their midst. As I gazed more and more at the overall scene, I realized one of the children was me, and the rest were friends of mine that had already passed on to the next world, playing in my hometown of Boulder, Colorado. I recognized that beautiful summer day. It was my birthday."

The angel next to her spoke and told her, "I've always been with you. I've always been here." Mildred recalled that when she was a child, she saw an angel, but no one believed her. As she grew older she had just failed to recollect. I wondered if Mildred was truly seeing her past, and, if so, if this was part of her life review.

Mildred had been raised Catholic, and was very meek and humble. Her husband had died a year before of a heart attack, and she was comforted by the knowledge that he was with Jesus and Mary. Six months after his death, he appeared to her in a repeated dream to tell her that they would be together, soon, forever. She was happy and ready to go with him. Mildred told me that her angel said that her dream was real and that this would occur soon, as there as not much to review with her because she had led a peaceful and joyful life with total love for God. The angel also told her that God was very proud of how she unconditionally loved her family and friends. Mildred had always felt bad for missing church, but she had always loved God deeply. Obviously God was more concerned about love. I always found it fascinating that those patients who strongly identified with God and desired to be with him appeared to have a swift and peaceful death. One thing was sure: Mildred was just taking pleasure in the visions and the experiences.

The sitters came and went, and they listened to me conversing with Mildred. One day, one of the sitters took me aside and asked me if we had a nurse on staff who dressed in an old-style nurse's uniform, with white shoes, white stockings, and an old-fashioned nurse's cap. I told her that I was not aware of anyone who still wore the traditional nurse's uniform, and asked why. She told me, "Well, this strikingly beautiful woman—almost radiant—walked in the early morning hours, opened a shiny book she had, and began to softly speak with Mildred. From what I could see, the book had lines and lines of names. Mildred opened her eyes, listened, and started talking to the nurse. As they were almost whispering, they appeared to be going down the lists in the book. After about 10 minutes, the nurse closed the book, kissed Mildred on the forehead, and walked out, saying, 'God is always with you.'"

Curious, the sitter reached out to touch her arm to ask her what they were talking about, but her hand went right through the nurse's body, which then walked straight through the closed door. By this time, there was nothing that could shock me when it came to Mildred. I replied, *"Is that why you asked me about the nurse?"*

"Yes. But also, I knew that I would not sound crazy telling you, because I see how you listen to Mildred's stories of angels with great interest. Dr. Lerma, when I ran to the door and opened it, I saw the angelic nurse go into the next room. I immediately went to the nurses' station and asked about the nurse in the old-time uniform. I described her, but the only two nurses present were not aware of any other nurse on duty." Making sure the patients were fine, they went to the room that the sitter had seen the mysterious nurse enter but found no one in the room except Joseph. He was quietly sleeping with a smile on his face.

The next day, I asked Mildred about the nurse. She responded, "That was an angel, and we were discussing people I knew who had passed on, and then we reviewed my married life. That's all I can tell you, Dr. Lerma. I'm sorry." Comforting her, I thanked her for her kindness and sincerity.

Continuing my daily rounds, I went into the next room to see Joseph, and, after my examination, I asked him if he remembered a nurse dressed in the old, traditional nurse's uniform visiting him last night. He squinted and asked why I wanted to know. I told him, *"Honestly, because there was a visitor who swears she saw an angelic nurse enter her room and then yours, and I was curious to know if you saw something like that."*

Joseph answered, "Yes, Dr. Lerma. There was this beautiful lady dressed like a nurse who prayed with me after asking me about my belief system. She said that I was in her book, and that she was going to help me get ready for my new and eternal life with God." Joseph went on to tell me how he was able to make amends with himself first and then his wife and children for abandoning them. He said he repented in the presence of Jesus Christ and was given the extra time to give his family closure and healing. Having been alienated from his family for more than 10 years, there had been no family visitors coming to see him. The social workers had been busy, but unsuccessful, in attempting to locate family members.

Joseph continued describing his encounter with the angel, how she was walking him through his whole life, and how the things that were bothering him were already in the book she carried. "Let me tell you, Dr. Lerma, what I learned from this angel and Jesus. You see, it is all about our free will, and without it God's perfect plan would never be realized. God was willing to die for us, so that free will could continue and so we always have the choice to proceed to its final completion: nirvana. The price was His life so as to give us 'seventy-seven times seven' chances to get it right. Without His death, we would self-destruct and enter an eternal nothingness. God knows we will veer off the straight and narrow path, and, for me, He knew the reality of the pain my choices caused me, but He allowed it, for in the end, the greater good would outweigh everything else. At the end, everything is perfected in our eyes, but in God's it was always perfect."

Joseph went on to say that he had to learn the lessons of alcoholism, including isolation and depression. His lessons also served to help his deceased mother and father, who had abandoned him as well. At the end of his conversation with the angel and Jesus, he was told the following: "Your wife and children will come to see you. We have angels working on that right now. The gift of unconditional love and opening their hearts to forgiveness is done, my son."

Two days before Joseph died, the social workers reached his family, who was devastated to hear the news. Because they lived in town, family members were able to come right away. I helped them understand what was happening, and told them about the remorse Joseph felt for abandoning them and that he wanted them to know he always thought of them and loved them. When they entered the room, he was so happy that he cried and cried, and repeatedly told them how much he loved them. It was just as the nurse and Jesus had told him it would be.

Joseph and Mildred were the only two patients who saw the nurse. I guess she was their guide to the other side. They were somehow connected. Joseph and Mildred died on the same day. Mildred died with a smile, very peacefully, and I was there when she passed. Her family was with her saying goodbye, loving her, and appreciating the lovely woman she had been. Joseph had his family with him, and he was filled with so much love that it was palpable.

The angelic nurse provided an amazing experience, but for me, the emotional and spiritual healings that took place at the end of life—of Mildred's and Joseph's immeasurably different lives—were a testament to God's true unconditional love.

Doctor's Notes and More Dialogue With Mildred

People who are in rooms next to each other often see the same visions, have some of the same experiences, and often die at the same time. It's also curious that sometimes people who have died in hospice have relatives who are assigned to the same room later on; I often see that. I've seen husbands and wives end up in the same room years apart, for example. At the time the staff assigns the rooms, a patient's history isn't known. Nurses report that certain rooms have specific energies and repeatedly attract the same kind of patient. Could it be that these rooms hold a specific type of electromagnetic energy? The hospice staff frequently hears eerie noises in certain rooms, such as deep, synchronous breathing (similar to that of a ventilator), even when no machine or patient is in the room. In other rooms, one might hear laughing or the sound of animals. It's as if the room is assigned to a particular experience and that it holds doorways to different dimensions with varying entities to help one with their life review. Mildred once said, "I wonder if you're not seeing, Dr. Lerma, because God works in my mind. He puts the picture in my mind. Or is it really out there, in the external environment?"

I told her, "*It's probably both ways. People see many kinds of visions.*"

She said, "God may be coming to them in their mind, too, or maybe we create our own reality."

As a scientist, I have come to believe that creation of our reality is how God works with us. That is possibly why every dying patient has different pictures of heaven. Heaven is what we have created in our mind, and this is what we look for as we are dying. God understands this and meets us in our created world to make the transition easier. With a physics background, I used to ponder if everyone else was seeing and experiencing what I was—and, if so, why? One theory was that human DNA consents to the same frequency of reality. As one dies, could it be that his or her DNA is dying and that the frequency channel of the body, if you will, is tuning the dial up or down, to a different reality? If that's the case, and our energy just changes form, then we will always exist. Mildred didn't ask the angels that question, but with a smirk said, "Does that really matter? The visions I received I knew were not from the devil or a negative frequency because they made me feel wonderful and exhilarated."

"Better than winning the lotto?" I asked.

"Dr. Lerma, better than all the margaritas in the world," Mildred answered, laughing almost uncontrollably. I really loved her!

My patients often see things in the corners. Mildred agreed: "It's always in the corners." Where corners meet seems to be a point of focus for entering this dimension. I asked Mildred if she felt any of the visions were from the dark side or the shadows, and she replied, "How can a shadow cause all those clear, bright colors? I know it's not that. The visions are full of so much love and peace that nothing would be overpowered by darkness."

Mildred was quite lucid and clear throughout most of our conversations; she knew her name, where she was, and what was happening at the time, and she could always recount the angelic visions and messages to the finest detail. She kept questioning her experiences, but in the end she defended them as being as real as her cancer. She would say, "Oh, my God. This is so real."

She said, "If there's no God and everyone is seeing this, how incredible our body is to make us experience this, that it could have been engineered at random to give us peace at our death. If randomness formed empathy and it was so specific, it's still an incredible experience. Funny how there were never living people in any of my angelic visions. Only the dead came to me. How can that be random?"

She continued, "It's awesome to know that loving God and my family was all that was needed to impress God. We think God wants so much more, where in reality, He just wants us to love Him and our family and ourselves. The rest comes easy. I lived a happy life. It's not about the size or quantity of things you do; caring for my children was more than enough. The angels showed me that my children will do great things, and that gives me joy and peace."

Mildred's son would become a lawyer and then a judge who would work to help victims of family violence. They showed her daughter with her children and the legacy of love they were passing on. She said, "It's like a relay race, where you have to pass the baton to your teammate, transferring your accomplishments; if one team member didn't do as well as he or she could have, then it was up to the next one to take up the slack. Many races can still be won as long as one person can take up the total slack. For the human race, that person is Jesus Christ. To win the race of life, we must love and teach our children total love and forgiveness, because it is through children, that the world will change."

I asked Mildred the question everyone wants to know: *"What is the meaning of life?"*

She answered, "I can't tell you what that is, for every soul has to figure that out for him or herself. However, I do recall a scripture the angels kept repeating as I was reviewing my life. This may help you find the answer." Opening the New Living Translation of the Bible, she read from Proverbs 2, verses 2–5:

> Tune your ears to wisdom,
> And concentrate on understanding.
> Cry out for insight,
> And ask for understanding.
> Search them as you would silver;
> Seek them like hidden treasures.
> Then you will understand what it means
> To fear the lord,
> And you will gain knowledge of God.

She said that the purpose of life is the same for all, as God and our individual spirits know, and that is to come to a closer understanding of God as all-loving, all-forgiving, and infinitely compassionate. He knows no negativity and desires only positive for us. She understood that hell does not exist in the way that man has made it out to be. It's a human projection that comes from fear. Fear leads you in a direction you don't want to go. To fear God is not the goal. To love God is the important thing. Separation from God is our hell. This darkness is within our human bodies, and it is up to us to invite God into our hearts so that He can curtail our evilness. It is a constant and daily effort that requires prayer. She said, "Now that I have experienced unconditional love through the angels, it would be hard to return to earth."

Chapter 8

Father Mike

Having just attended the noon services at the hospital chapel, I received a page that a well-respected and well-loved Catholic priest was to be transferred to our palliative unit for terminal care. I was honored that I was being asked to care for a man who had willfully and with total love given his life to carry out God's plan on earth. (Raised in a Catholic family, I have great respect for the church and for priests.) Father Mike was a 78-year-old retired priest who had been the president of a Catholic university. He was a brilliant and compassionate man with a reputation for living his beliefs. He was diagnosed with head and neck cancer a year before he arrived at our hospice facility, and had a second primary diagnosis of lung cancer. The advanced nature of his illness did not respond to aggressive therapies, and so he was finally referred to hospice. Upon his transfer to our pain-management facility, he was emaciated and in intense pain. Father Mike was missing one eye, and the remaining eye had severe cataracts. Considering his condition, he was in good spirits and very talkative, although his voice was hoarse from the cancer.

Father Mike made it enormously clear when we first met that his desire was to feel his pain in its most raw form. As a pain specialist, that was both an inconceivable request and tremendous conflict for me. I felt that it violated my oath to do no harm, not to mention the ethical dilemma. Fortunately, the Self-Determination Act of 1990 and the ethical principle of autonomy ensured patients of sound mind and body their rights in determining their choice regarding medical treatments and other health issues. After several days of interacting with him while he suffered in terrific pain, he asked for another physician to take over his case. He felt that I was too empathetic and that I might override his orders to be allowed to experience his grief. He asked me to continue to talk to him, however, about what the pain was teaching him.

Father Mike understood my heartfelt desire to help him and was overwhelmed with my enthusiasm to relieve human suffering. Because he had taught a subject on the importance of suffering for spiritual freedom at the university, I asked him if he would not mind sharing his insight with me. He was delighted, and thus began my two weeks of what appeared to be a university course on the positive effects of pain by a renowned theologian. I was honored to have this opportunity to be part of what I felt to be Father Mike's last earthly class. He laughed as he told me to take notes, as there would be a test in the next few days to weeks.

Father Mike began by instructing me on Opus Dei's beliefs with regard to pain and suffering. He agreed that these acts of suffering would help countless souls around the world, including our hospice patients. He said he would suffer for me.

I felt so loved with his offering, but I assured him I did not want to add to his burden. Father Mike insisted that I trust the spiritual process. At that point, his prognosis was five to 10 days, and he was already seeing angels and fellow priests who had passed on. He told me the comfort they presented. Honestly, I was more interested in his visions at that point, so I asked questions about the apparitions: what they looked like, who else was present, and what their purpose was. He said that several Archangels were in his presence. The larger angels came in to protect him while he negotiated to take on physical and emotional pain. There was that word again: *negotiating*.

He continued, "During deep pain, you become vulnerable to darkness. The angels protect me from veering away from my goal of selflessly giving this gift to the world." The angels were supportive of and uplifted him. To lift Father Mike's spirits, there were times they would reveal the positive effects his suffering—which had now turned to joy—was having on humanity. That gave him the strength to continue. I asked if his pain was unbearable. He answered with a resounding, "Yes, but believe it or not I feel nothing but adulation and joy, for God. You know something? I guess my pain was converted to joy. Isn't God the best?!"

"Absolutely, Father Mike. God is the best," I told him.

When I told him about our precious Matthew, who had said the same thing, Father Mike said, "That little boy was probably a highly spiritual soul. Children do tremendous good when they die early and willingly suffer pain." He also said that children do not have to be sick to see angels. They are more closely connected with the angelic realm than adults.

At one point I noted that he was exhibiting all the physical signs of severe pain, yet he remained steadfast in his decision to release it to God and was translating it to joy and love, the two key ingredients to create miracles. *"Father Mike, you said you needed to feel pain to help the world. Well, if God is removing your pain, then how does that help?"*

He answered, "The pain does not have to be physical pain. Spiritual pain is the real suffering. In the end, it's really not suffering. Suffering from a spiritual standpoint is really joy. The easiest way to explain it to you, Dr. Lerma, is through an analogy of science and physics. The raw energy of true joy and true spiritual pain only differs by an electrical charge, if you will: pain with a negative charge, and joy with a positive one.

"To remove pain, one can choose to use pain medications to mask it, or one can choose to physically change the molecule's radical charge. You essentially bombard the particle with opposite charges and get the end result of its counterpart or antimatter. This is too complicated for humans to accomplish, so one has let go of our pain and concerns, and let God do the rest. Again, it's all about free will. God will love us the same, no matter what decision we make. Bottom line: One can only understand joy if one experiences pain. Both these emotional experiences bring us to God." I was astounded at his scientific explanation. On some level it really made sense.

I wanted to know more about the entities he called angels, so I asked him to describe what they were doing, saying, and so forth. Father Mike said, "That's a good idea. Let's talk about these beautiful creatures of God and their powers. In terms of how they look—well, that changes. You see, the angels can change the way they look, including their colors. Apparently, the emotions of people in the room seem to affect this process. With me, when I was having a difficult time with my illness, their light dimmed. The angels would swiftly lift my spirits by radiating love towards my heart. Within a few minutes, I brightened up and so did they. The majority of the time, I was full of joy and excitement that I was able to do something positive for the entire world, before I died." It was still difficult for me to watch his pain. "Dr. Lerma, the angels, at their highest level of love, appeared fiercely white."

I thought how this agreed with the science of photon energy, where the higher energies give off the most light. Father Mike continued, "There is a spectrum of light from gold to yellow to blues to green, from pink to purple. The colors are so much more brilliant and radiant than earth's color spectrum. This light floats around all of us, but with varying intensities. Dr. Lerma, your aura is gold right now, and that exudes peace and love." I was surprised to hear a Catholic priest talking about auras.

He told me that, when he first saw me and I connected with his pain, my aura was a dull color, because I was letting his pain control me. He taught me that I have to see people's diseases and their pain—physical, spiritual, social, or emotional—on all levels as being needed for their lessons while relieving their pain. It helps them come closer to God and to understand the interconnectedness of all things in this world. "Dr. Lerma, God has allowed you to have a passion to reduce suffering, and God wants you to continue do it on all levels and elucidate this form of medicine to other physicians. Doctors need to learn to treat the mind, body, spirit, and family, so that, through their compassion and loving words, healing for the entire family is possible. Dr. Lerma, this type of medicine will help bring peace to the world."

"Father Mike, was reincarnation discussed by the angels?" I asked.

"No, but anything is possible with God. The angels discuss the importance of this life with regard to our eternal survival with God. For me, I have a strong need to finish this life's mission: to live the life I preached and taught. If the main reason to reincarnate is to finish lessons and make amends, I believe our God of love would allow lessons to be learned in the next world. For Catholics, we believe this place is purgatory. For others there is hell."

"Father Mike, what about hell? Is this God's answer to dealing with those that refused to learn their lessons, or who committed unforgivable sins?"

"Now this they did discuss. They affirmed a dark side, but it is unlike what man perceives it to. Hell is the soul's willful separation from the light of God. God never leaves his creation and the book of Psalms asserts this in chapter 139, verses 7–8:

> I can never escape from your spirit!
> I can never get away from your presence!
> If I go up to heaven you are there;
> If I go down to hell, you are there.

In fact, with eternity on his side, he will work on getting those guilt-ridden souls to learn to forgive themselves and then to love themselves. Once this is done, the soul chooses to move toward the light of God—Heaven. God is pure love! We are not! We create our hell, not God. God creates the way out of hell. They said that mankind's not going to Hell. He or she is already in hell. We are trying to depart from it. God and the angels were concerned that mankind are now exposed more often to people's sins than to their goodness, and this increases our ability to sin. For example, watching the negative aspects of world and local news affects our souls in a dark way, and puts us in a position to develop fear and judgment of others, without even trying. This compounds the negativity in our souls and this truly hurts God. The angels I spoke with talked about working on many projects to improve optimism in the world. One of those was to increase the number of workers in the entertainment and news that are God-loving."

By this point, I was so mesmerized with his information that I did not even know what to ask. So he said, "Let's talk about peace."

"That sounds great," I answered. *"How can God continue to unfold in an era where famine, disasters, and disease appear to go unchecked?"*

"Good question. I have already answered most of it, and I want you to think about and understand what I told you about suffering."

I asked for more specifics. He said, "It's specific and it's general, but it's through peace, love, and technology that will help us address the issues of war, famine, and diseases—technology integrated with spirituality. God has given us the gift of technology, but we have turned away from our spirituality. Technology has made things worse in the short term because spirituality is not integrated. We're in a big mess now because we haven't stepped up to the plate. But that will change. There are individuals who come in with assignments to take on all the darkness that is caused by our leaders, our armies, or whoever abuses technology and science. By doing this, it affects generational sin. Eventually those people will die. By accepting suffering now, I am helping their spirits get rebalanced."

I asked how that happens, and Father Mike explained, "We hold these spirits in love and balance them out. It is because of those people who volunteer to suffer for others in joy that this world has not been destroyed. We are always on the brink, but a few people keep raising the level of humanity." He used the example of the Cuban Missile Crisis that went down to the last minute. He said there was a high amount of prayer, and, through that prayer, our spirit woke up just in time to prevent devastation. Random acts of kindness can actually stop wars from occurring, and just one unconditional act of love can change the entire world.

"God has unfolded our technology and it has grown exponentially over the recent years." When I asked him why God did this, he replied, "To make our lives happier and boundless."

I asked, "*What do we learn from that?*"

"To love one another and to learn interconnectedness. By doing so, we can propel each other to a level of ultimate love where anything is possible. Technology without the spirit can actually destroy us. In fact, that has happened before." He said that the Roman Empire is an example of this. He told me that Christ came to prevent the total destruction of the soul.

Through His willful suffering and death, we were forgiven, and mankind was saved from annihilation. That is why it was so important for Jesus to have come at that time. As the angels have said before, we were at critical mass with the decision of continuing or starting over.

I asked about Atlantis and he said, "We've done this many times, and we've had to start over. But this time one man changed the entire world."

"How can we avoid this in the future?"

He replied, "We can follow the example of Christ, through prayer, knowledge, and self-sacrifice, and through collective love and joy."

In the following days, Father Mike became weaker and had a more difficult time speaking. Father Mike felt he had revealed as much as I needed to know about pain and suffering, as well as other important factors. He said that I was in the right place doing what I needed to do. He said that my sacrifice and my joy would be to watch thousands of people die and to help guide them joyfully to the other side.

He slipped into a coma three days before he died and was still not receiving pain medication. He was short of breath, but he had an incredible glow and peace about him. His heart rate was higher than one hundred and thirty, signifying distress, but he remained at peace with a large smile.

On the day he died, I was at my clinic across the street, and, as the sky darkened, I looked out the window and saw a dark cloud over the hospital where Father Mike was, and it began to storm, beginning with gale-force type winds, then hail, and finally rain. As the storm intensified, I received a page that Father Mike had passed and that I needed to come immediately.

I rushed across the street, getting drenched and windblown. As I arrived at the hospice unit, the lights on the hospice floor were flickering on and off. There was an incredible sense of peace in the midst of the chaos that was occurring. Several nurses and my secretary were present. They had rushed me there to experience an inconceivable event. Every time the lights turned on and off, little feathers fell from the ceiling, drifting down as if they were snowflakes. One fell in the hand of a nurse and disappeared. As soon as they fell, they disappeared. Father Mike's call light was going off and on. His door, which had been closed when he died, was now open. The secretary and one nurse saw a bright light shining from his room. They thought the lights were coming back on, but the bright light was radiating from his body or bed. Out of that light came this bright sphere that floated out of his body and circled the bed about three times before it soared out of the closed window. Less than a minute later, the lights came back on, it stopped raining, and all the feathers disappeared. We all had goose bumps.

It was about four in the afternoon when I entered the room to pronounce him. Father Mike had a striking smile on his face, his palms were open, and the eye that had the cataract seemed to have cleared. He looked so peaceful—blissful almost.

Some of us questioned his choice to suffer, but that experience, in the end, taught us to respect our patients' wishes. Everyone who was there that afternoon experienced these miraculous events. We could try to explain that the lights had something to do with the storm, but the feathers were unexplainable.

The priests and the nuns came in from the university later that afternoon. The new dean described something similar that occurred in their offices during the storm. Lights turned off and then on, and a few feathers were found on the floor after the storm. Most of them, who knew how spiritual and God-loving Father Mike was, sensed at that moment that he had died. The dean went on to say that Father Mike had collected feathers all his life, and he always said, whenever he found feathers, that they were angel feathers. He had a large glass bottle filled with feathers from all over the world that he had found. After the incident in their offices, the dean went into Father Mike's office and noticed that all the feathers from the jar were gone. He said Father Mike always said he would give them a sign when his mission was accomplished. What better sign than raining angel feathers?

Doctor's Notes and More Dialogue With Father Mike

Father Mike and I had many discussions, and one of the most profound for me was regarding the age of wisdom. He said wisdom is the key to our survival—survival of the wisest, not survival of the fittest. He said that we have reached the level where we have the technology and skills to solve all our social problems. He said, "Imposing our beliefs on others causes the dark side of our souls to awaken. It is this part of us that is stimulated by fear, anger, and resentment, and, once aroused, it will not retreat easily."

Father Mike said we have to transcend racial intolerance to create world peace. He was in agreement with Einstein, who said that nationalism is like measles to humanity. As a human race, we are in danger of becoming extinct, because the financially and physically strong have been allowed to impose their will on others. Even one human soul with tyrannical ideas and vast power can lead a small or large group of people to overtake a society for better or for worse, as Hitler or Gandhi did, in opposite extremes. "This phase of mankind will come to an end once we decide to collectively redirect our energy and our egos to solve the problems of famine, illness, and global warming. The technology and understanding are accessible. All we have to do is decide to just do it. It is during this period that the age of wisdom will commence, and love and peace will secure our eternal existence with God."

Father Mike said once this idea reaches critical mass, we can change as a group, through our "imaginal selves." Father Mike said, "Like a caterpillar, we have these dormant cells within us, called imaginal cells, which, once activated, will undergo metamorphosis and create a mind, body, and spirit change, just as the butterfly is the changed caterpillar. We, like the monarch, will become free to experience and become one with the universe. At this point, we become co-creators with Christ, who lives within each one of us. He is the 'imaginal self' within us." Of interest, imaginal cells in the caterpillar are responsible for its metamorphosis. How incredible would that be for our bodies to have such cells that have to be inspired to cause change? Could it be the Word of God that fuels this positive change?

It is collective wisdom that brings understanding of who we are and why we do what we do. Through this collective understanding of consciousness, we will know that peace is the only way to prevent our extinction and secure our future. We have reached several critical masses in our existence. When the comet hit Jupiter in 1994, any one of those fragments could have destroyed the world. Scientists began looking for comets and asteroids headed in our direction, and of great concern was a large asteroid that was found to have a trajectory toward Earth. Fortunately, it is still several hundred years away from a probably collision with our planet, giving us ample time to determine how best to re-direct its path. Nuclear bombs will not destroy it, but just disperse massive fragments. Technology or thought will progress to take care of that challenge only if we achieve where we need to be in the next several hundred years.

Hopefully, we will take Father Mike's advice and cultivate spirituality and technology together. Father Mike inspired this stream of consciousness for me and activated the information within me, and I am forever changed because of it.

Chapter 9

Heaven in Room 212

I sat on the side of the bed talking to Joanna on her first day at hospice. She was only 28 and suffering from advanced breast cancer. I asked what her concerns were, and she laughed, and asked, "Other than dying?"

I smiled at her humor and said, *"Yes, other than dying. Can you think of anything you want me to do for you?"*

She heaved a deep sigh, and suddenly her smile changed to a look of great sadness. "I have three children and essentially no family: 6-year-old Elizabeth, 8-year-old Camille, 10-year-old Daniel, and one cousin, Robin, who's 18 years old and whose parents were murdered during the war in Somalia. Robin will probably end up taking care of my children, which I know is not the best situation, but what choice do I have?" Robin was young, was married with one child of her own, and lived below poverty level.

I asked if she had any contact with the children's fathers and she replied, "There were two men, the father of my first two children and the father of the third. I was only married to the first gentleman and just lived with the second man." I asked her about the men, and whether either of them would possibly be willing to take on the father role. "Dr. Lerma, because both were not involved in the children's lives, it was difficult to say. However, I remember my ex-husband being very caring but immature, and the second had been involved with drugs at the time. It's been years since I have been in contact with them. If I had a choice, I would love to have my ex-husband care for all three of the children. I do not want them to be separated, Dr. Lerma. You know what you can do for me? You can pray with me and ask God to find a loving and secure household for my babies." I held her hand and said the Lord's Prayer. After reciting the prayer with intense fervor, I promised her I would work diligently with the help of our social workers, to locate her ex-husband. "I know God will lead you to him. Thank you, Dr. Lerma." I passed the data along to our team, who began the search.

As I managed Joanna's pain, she began to relax and gain some peace. It was now one week since our search commenced, and, despite reassurance that her children would be cared for, she began to lose hope and enter a depressive state. As is the case with most other patients at this stage, depression fed the guilt, which further increased her existential and emotional distress. By this time no amount of opiates could ease her pain, as it was largely spiritual. Our chaplains and ministers did not cease from comforting her with God's promise of forgiveness and love, but she was convinced that her current circumstances were consequences of her past sins.

She believed in God's forgiveness, but ironically she could not forgive God, her father, or herself. I asked her what was so horrible that would cause such anger. She said, "I can not forgive myself because I can not forget and forgive the men I loved with all my soul."

"How is that possible, Joanna?" I asked, as I could almost palpate her conflict. *"How can you not forgive someone you deeply loved?"*

With tears rolling down her cheeks, she answered, "That's easy when it's people you love without trying, like my father and God."

Sitting on the edge of her bed and holding her hand securely, I asked, *"What have they done to cause this conflict within you?"*

"Dr. Lerma, my father always loved me so much and he taught me God would always love us and always protect us. I remember my daddy playing dolls with me, taking me to school, and cooking for my friends and me. I would invite them over for slumber parties."

"How about your mother and siblings?" I asked.

Joanna said that her mother had died of breast cancer just a year after she was born. Evidently, her mother was diagnosed with this malignancy during her third trimester and decided to avert any treatment that would potentially harm her child, at least until she was born. "My daddy said that my mother was a beautiful, God-loving woman who helped the poor and the needy. It was not uncommon to have homeless women living in their home. She would offer them a place to live and eat with no more required than a chance to hear God's word and a desire to improve their lives. Ultimately, she was responsible for starting a refuge for homeless women, which to date has helped thousands of woman come to know God and attain an education.

"I would love to have known my mom. Given that my mother died one year after I was born and I was her only child, I lost the opportunity of having brothers and sisters. My daddy tried hard to take my mother's place and, to me, he did a great job at being both parents. He never let me forget that he was only a father and that my mom was helping from the spiritual world. We became best friends. He taught me how to read and write, ride a bike, roller skate, change a flat tire, and even pray. Yes, my dad and I were church-going people, and we even joined the choir. Those times were so much fun. I was the luckiest girl around.

"When I would ask about my mom, my daddy would always speak highly of her and was never angry at God for taking her at such an early age. I was a reflection of my father; I, too, exuded forgiveness and unconditional love. As I became a teenager, my relationship with my father grew, as well as my emotions. These hormonal periods somehow fostered a feeling of insecurity. With tears in my eyes, I frequently asked my daddy if God would take him while I was still very young. He promised me that God would only take him when I was all grown up, married, and responsible for my own children. His constant reassurance brought peace into my heart. I was once again on top of the world.

"When I turned 16, my father planned a great church celebration in honor of my becoming a woman. I shared his gratitude to God for all the wonderful years and blessings He had bestowed on us. After the church service, my dad and I decided to walk home, only six blocks away. After all, it was a beautiful autumn evening and houses were being decorated for Halloween. Walking down the church steps, we both heard police sirens approaching and saw several police cars pursuing a pick-up truck. As they speeded passed us, I heard gunfire being exchanged. Frightened, we quickly fell to the ground. The cars passed, and all that remained were the smell of exhaust fumes, smoke, and a large pool of blood around my dad's head. My daddy had been shot!

"I screamed so loud that people inside the church that had not heard the police sirens and the loud gunshots quickly responded. I held my daddy close to my chest and was drenched in blood; the paramedics had to almost pry him from me. I was in utter shock. He was taken to the hospital, where a neurosurgeon was waiting. After six hours of surgery, the doctor, looking quite distressed, told me that my father had fought hard. He was pronounced dead at 11:30 in the evening. The gunshot wound caused massive brain trauma. Even if had lived, he would be left in a vegetative state. At that moment I remember thinking that it was the best and worst day of my life. 'How could this senseless accident happen?' I asked.

"I immediately became so angry at my father for leaving me and at God for taking him, especially after the promise made by my father. I was so infuriated with God for not only taking my mother and my unborn siblings, but for taking my father and our dreams for our life. Where was I to go from here? Who would care for me and learn to love me? Would he or she fall to the same fate?

"I decided then never to let anyone into my heart and vice versa. I knew this was the only way I could survive this life and keep from hurting myself and others. At times I felt I was being punished by God and, more often than not, that there really was no loving God. I could not help but think that we were all alone to fend for ourselves." As I listened to her heartfelt account, I could not help but want to save her by finding the right words that would miraculously remove her emotional and spiritual pain. The truth was that there were no words or potions to make it all better. There were only my love and empathy. So, I continued listening and caressing her forehead.

"I moved in with Robin and continued school. After graduating from high school, I met a college boy named Daniel, who I fell deeply in love with. He seemed to have some of the characteristics of my father as well as a love for God. This was truly a miracle. We moved in together, and within the year I was pregnant. Without delay, we married, only to be divorced three years and two children later. It was quickly apparent that the loss of my parents, which left me bitter and fearful, outweighed my love for Daniel. Therefore, I unknowingly sabotaged the relationship to keep from feeling the pain of another loss. My life was a double-edged sword; I was my worst enemy. Afterward, I fell into a deep depression with thoughts of suicide. I could not act on those thoughts as I had two beautiful children that depended on me. The internal conflict was intense.

"With no money or home, I prostituted myself to a man who was willing to provide a home for my children and me, in exchange for favors. The relationship ended six months later, and I was left to face the world with my two beautiful children and another on the way. This time I did not have to sabotage the relationship. The heroin he was selling accomplished that. He was arrested for selling heroin and sentenced to 20 years in the penitentiary. This time God was second to the justice and penal system. Either way, I was on my own again.

"I moved back in with my cousin and decided to get a degree in nursing so I could care for my children and myself. Six months after having my third child, a beautiful baby girl named Elizabeth, I entered college. Juggling school, my three children, and part-time work at the college, I noticed that I was losing weight and becoming increasingly weak. I explained it as stress from school and home. The symptoms worsened and, one morning while in class, I fainted. I was rushed to the hospital, where I was admitted with severe dehydration and unexplained weight loss. After five days of blood tests, X-rays, CAT scans, and MRIs, a deep mass on my left breast was found. A biopsy was performed, and within two days I was told I had breast cancer of an aggressive type that had metastasized to my spine, ribs, pelvis, liver, and brain. My cousin, who had been caring for my children, was visibly frightened by the prospect of losing me and having to care for my three children as well as her own. I was overwhelmed, devastated, and grief-stricken. Who would care for Elizabeth, Camille, and Daniel? They were my life and I theirs.

"By this point I had lost more than one hundred pounds, now only weighing 88 pounds with a height of 5 feet 7 inches. Chemotherapy and radiation were initiated, but had to be stopped because they further injured my kidney and liver. I was placed on dialysis, but my organ systems continued to shut down. The oncologist recommended halting any further aggressive treatments, as they was futile and would hasten my death. Hospice and palliative care were recommended."

Joanna agreed to stop all forms of aggressive treatments including dialysis. Her prognosis was one to two weeks. Sobbing, she told me that God was continuing His morbid vendetta against her and her children. Joanna stated, "God is taking the only three things I adore in this painful and cruel world: my children. I will not succumb to this life until I know that my children are placed in a loving home."

Within 24 hours of making her decision for comfort care, Joanna was transferred to our inpatient hospice unit, where her terminal symptoms could be effectively managed. After listening to her heartbreaking story, I knew I had to do whatever it took to help her find the peace, trust, and unconditional love she once proclaimed for God and the world. With her pain adequately controlled and more alert, Joanna was able to give the hospice team the needed information to locate her ex-husband. Over the next few days, with no urine output and having been off dialysis for five days, Joanna began to decline rapidly. She was noticeably thinner, weaker, depressed, and increasingly short of breath from increasing pulmonary edema.

By that time, we had found that the father of the third child was still in prison, and years from being released. As for Daniel, he had remarried and moved out of state, but we were unable to find his address. Joanna was not immediately told of these difficulties, for fear of increasing her social, emotional, and spiritual pain. As do many patients with a three- to five-day prognosis, Joanna started describing visions of her deceased parents and other spiritual beings. I knew from experience that this meant that her death was very close. Wondering if these were chemically induced visual hallucinations or delirium from uremia, I found it interesting that her cognitive function was quite clear for the first time in one week; she was oriented to her name, the date, the place, and specific dates in American history, and she was able to recall complicated phrases.

It was clear that Joanna had total understanding and clarity of the situation, and was not having hallucinations. She started recounting observing a large rainbow in the room with a multitude of brilliant and iridescent colors piercing the walls, ceilings, and floors, and our bodies, particularly our chests. From the rainbow, one large, bright, white sphere was ejected into the middle of the room, only to divide into about 20 to 30 other smaller spheres. The process released so much white light that Joanna said our bodies were no longer visible except a dark blue golden color coming from my chest, and a violet golden and a soft pink color emanating from Robin's chest. Joanna said this was the light energy from our souls tying together. I asked her, *"Why different colors?"*

She was told that each color shares a frequency with God and that it is up to all of us to commune together and work together because two or more colors together can start to form a rainbow that summons Him. "In the room right now, there are more than five human-colored frequencies that are so bright and unified: two nurses, my cousin, you, and me. When two or more are gathered with evil thoughts, the color is black and thus draws everyone's colors of love, leaving them feeling drained. This is why the color black is so hot in the summer. It attracts all the colors in the spectrum."

She went on to say that we need to protect our soul's energy from those people who consume your energy and place you at risk for health and spiritual problems. "Through unconditional acts of love and kindness, as well as healthy forms of laughter, exercise, nutrition, and strength in prayer, one can help those that are weaker. Even Jesus had to be re-energized by God quite frequently so He could continue to help the sick of mind, body, and spirit, and often would gravitate to His soul light for sustenance." After the light disseminated, there were about 20 spheres, which transformed into her father, her mother, and many other beings she called angels. She described her parents as being human in appearance and around their late 20s to early 30s.

The angels were of varying colors and sizes, and different personalities. Two or three angels were the most beautiful color of Aegean blue and about 7 feet tall with a jovial, witty attitude. They were making her laugh by tickling her soul with their feathers. Others were pure white and so large that their wings were in a forward position and hugging all of us in the room including the other angels. "Their eyes were iridescent, blue to green colors I've never seen," she described. "They pierced my very soul and filled me with God's love and peace. Whatever they looked at took on God's love and peace, and it gleamed with joy." She saw the angels look at the nurses, her cousin, and me, and saw an enormous aura around us that was connected to the rainbow. Still other angels were frolicking and flying around the room and through our bodies. Joanna said, "Look, Dr. Lerma. They are flying through your heart and soul. Don't you feel it and see them?"

"No, Joanna, but I wish I did." Strangely, I did feel static energy in the room. I had no goose bumps, but the hairs on my arm and head were partially erect. As I looked over to my nurse, she agreed that she felt the static as well. Was it just our response to her incredible story, or were we in the midst of another dimension with the liberation of electrical energy? By this time, Joanna was exhilarated and in ecstasy. She was praising God again!

I asked her what her parents were doing and saying. She answered in a loving voice, "They are caressing my hair and whispering in my ears. They are explaining so many things that would help me leave my body with ease."

"What is needed to separate from our earthly bodies?" I asked.

"It's different for everyone, but what I can say is that everyone will be given the answer key to all our questions and more. Part of our life review is to understand the answers to the questions we always asked while on earth. The more questions one asks about God and the creation of the universe, including life, love, and death, and attempts to find these answers by reading and communing with other humans, the further one's understanding of God will be, thus assuring an easier life review. Essentially, one has to pass a sort of test before moving forward. Passing this life review test involves understanding why we sinned and sensing the remorse, and developing the skills of unconditional love and forgiveness. The inability to develop these gifts results in a type of failure.

In other words, one has to go to a special place to work on those inadequacies. One on earth would call this hell; however, it involves all higher souls to aid in their learning. After all, on the other side, one is full of love and automatically wants to help these poor souls."

With regard to her life review, Joanna said that all the answers to her questions were given with love and peace, and it all finally made sense: The more loving one is on earth and the more random acts of kindness one performs, the easier it will be to forgive oneself and thus move into harmony with God. I asked why God allows pain, suffering, and murders. She explained that, to understand why God allows this would take eons, but it is somewhat explained via God's gift of free will to man: "Free will is at the core of why the universe, elements, planets, stars, and animals were created. All for us. Surrounding all of this is God."

Faith, she was told, is what connects the two: "Without faith, our free will will float freely like an oxide radical, bonding to anything other than God for support. Some might call this our dark side. Having free will connect to our weaker side that separates us from God's knowledge and thus automatically brings about questions, usually negative in nature, and with their answers coming from other humans with no positive connection. This leads to confusion and pride. To avert this, humans were given the opportunity to find explanations from humans filled with God's spirit and His word. Everyone is given an infinite number of chances to seek the light, which is connected by faith to God, the infinite supplier of all answers. It is only this way that we learn to depend on the supernatural abilities of Jesus."

Joanna stated that her intense pain associated with the death of her parents, then her divorce, and eventually her terminal illness were acknowledged by God to be extremely painful. God understood her anger and her separation from Him; however, He never left her side. She explained, "I left His side emotionally. The questions that were coming from my dark side were so intense that, by not choosing faith to answer it, the only other option was anti-faith. The darkness within me was now answering its own questions and becoming pride-filled and further destructive. Eventually, the majority of my soul energy turned negative, and illness and further problems were manifested. God said all our choices have consequences, but He is always here to console us. We must remember that true peace is governed by God's law of attraction. When negative attracts negative, be it oneself or other humans, the result is devastating. One must continue to fight to learn from our faithless (negative) side, by connecting to our faithful (positive) side, which is connected to God."

Joanna wanted me to tell as many people as I could that all humans will at one time or another in their life feel anger and hatred towards themselves, others, or God. Joanna said, "Never cease from asking God for the answer, and do this with as much peace and love as you can rally. Do not rely on Godless people or our dark side to lead us. It will always fail us. Just look at history."

Next, she saw that the original large sphere reappeared and took the form of Jesus. The angels announced His presence, and all gravitated towards Him and entered His heart. At that moment, Jesus exuded an incredibly bright white light, with a multitude of shimmering colors emanating from His heart. He told Joanna that Daniel would care for her three children, as she had prayed. She was shown the messenger angel that was sent to the children's father to place a feeling of love and longing for his children and ex-wife. She was told that this would occur that day, as she was ready to leave her body and enter heaven. At that moment, her cousin ran out of the room crying, suspecting that she was within minutes of dying.

Joanna sat up, raised her almost-paralyzed arms toward the direction where Jesus appeared, and sang "Glory Hallelujah" to Jesus, who she said was kneeling at the floor of her bed. Just after the song, she sat back in her bed, looked up, and fell asleep with a big smile. Just then, a social worker paged me to the nurse's station. The social worker had just hung up the phone with a man named Daniel, who said he was the father of two of the children, and he wanted to come and help. I remarked, *"It's a miracle. Joanna said we would find him, and we did."*

He was in Michigan. Daniel told the social worker that he always loved Joanna, but having a job making only four dollars per hour and having to care for two children and a wife overwhelmed him. In his 30s, he finally matured and looked for Joanna, but he heard she was living with another man and in love. Daniel said, "Fearing that I lost her for good, I moved on. A year ago, I met Esther, a loving and devoutly Christian woman. We married within the year, and she was the reason I searched for Joanna. Esther is pediatric nurse who started a non-profit program for orphans prior to our meeting."

Daniel explained that two days earlier, an angel came to him in a dream and told him that Joanna was dying and that she needed him. He said it was so vivid. He recounted the dream to Esther, who pressed him to locate Joanna and the children. He immediately started the search and reached one of Joanna's and his mutual friends, who revealed the news about Joanna's illness. Daniel apologized to the social worker for his lack of involvement.

The next day, he showed up and knelt at Joanna's bedside. He told her he was sorry that he had abandoned them, and that he and his wife would take care of all three children. Daniel told Joanna not to worry, and that he would love them and so would his wife. It was heartfelt and moving. Amazingly, Joanna opened her eyes and smiled at him. She said, "It's beautiful. It's so beautiful! Is this what heaven looks like? There are mountains and bright green grass; the colors are so brilliant. There are angels; beautiful blue, white and pink, whizzing through the room, moving right through your soul and through my cousin and me." Again, she looked ecstatic as she reached for my hand and said, "Don't you feel it, Dr. Lerma?"

I answered, *"No, I wish I could feel it. Would you tell me where my soul is?"*

She laid her palm against my chest and said, "Right there. In your heart and right through your chest." Joanna then stretched her right arm up toward the ceiling as if someone were taking her hand, and said, "I'm ready to go. I'm happy now." She smiled a beautiful smile as she closed her eyes for the last time, and she whispered, "It's brighter and more beautiful than ever."

Daniel put his arms around Robin and the children, and they cried for Joanna's early death. I knew some of those tears were for joy, because Daniel had made amends and was now ready and able to take care of the children, and because the angels had brought them together at just the right time.

Doctor's Notes

When I met Daniel, I instinctively recognized a family resemblance, as well as the same deep-rooted compassion for life. All three children looked so much alike, yet two resembled him more than Joanna. I suggested that they take paternity tests. It turned out only the first two were his, but the similarity was uncanny. The children and their father were filled with joy at hearing the wonderful news that they were going to have a daddy and mommy who were going to keep them all together. With tears in the children's eyes, they said, "Now we have our daddy, and we will never be separated." I knew then what Joanna had negotiated with the angels, and once again I was mystified by God's incredible compassion and love.

I followed up one year later with the family and found the children, their father, and their new mom to be the epitome of a loving and spiritual family. As for me, I went home, hugged my children, and told them how much God and I loved them.

Chapter 10

MiMi and the Confirmation

I was paged to Room 111 by Leila, the daughter of MiMi, an 81-year-old woman who was dying of kidney failure. I rushed over, as I knew she was close to death. When I entered the room, nothing seemed to be out of order except that Leila and her family appeared as though they had seen a ghost. MiMi was a non-denominational Christian from Lakewood Church. When she was awake, I had experienced her as a kind and loving matriarch who had an immense love for her grandchildren. She begged for them to come as often as they could, so they would remember her when she was gone.

Leila began to describe an amazing, mystical story that was occurring in the room, and it frightened her, thinking she was about to lose her mother. "Don't think I'm crazy, Dr. Lerma, but this is what is happening. My two children were playing on the floor earlier and Bobby Joe, who is 3, and Joanie, who is 4, saw something that was invisible to me. They are lovely children who seldom fight and play so well together, unlike so many siblings." I asked Leila what was wrong, and she suggested that I sit and observe the children.

I sat down across the room so I wouldn't disturb their play and just observed what was happening. Within 10 minutes, the children got up and walked to the corner of the room, near the windows that face the garden. The little girl, Joanie, seemed to be holding hands with someone. All I noticed was the bright sunlight from the outside that was shining directly on Joanie. This was odd, because, by this time of day, the sun was already on the other side of the building. Joanie turned to her mom and said, "Mommy, isn't this the most beautiful golden angel?" She looked from the floor up to the ceiling, and said, "It's so enormous, but gentle, and I love it when it closes its wings around me. The feathers tickle me." She giggled as if she were being tickled at that moment. "My angel told me not to be afraid, and I'm not afraid. I'm a big girl."

Bobby Joe said, "My angel's blue, because I'm a boy." He looked proudly up and down from the floor to the ceiling, too. "Is it true, Mommy? Is MiMi really going to leave us?"

"Why do you say that, Bobby?" Leila asked him.

"Because that's what the blue angel is telling me, but he says not to be sad." Bobby pointed to the corner and said, "Hi, MiMi. You look so pretty in that white dress. Do you have a lightbulb inside you?" After his question, he walked closer to the corner of the room and hugged what seemingly was empty space. He then turned his head sideways as if he was leaning against something. Bobby looked so elated.

Looking anxious, Leila walked toward me and whispered in my ear, "Is this really happening?"

"Leila, I am as mystified as you are. Have your children ever spoken about an invisible friend?"

"Not that I know. I doubt it, Dr. Lerma. They always play with each other and would not have a need to make up a friend. My mother always told me that children are so innocent and that they can see angels and people from the heaven. Maybe that's what's happening here."

Because they were in no danger, I told her to let them continue their experience, as this could be a coping mechanism. *"Why don't I have the psychologist speak with them later and discuss their experience? I'll make sure they are counseled and comforted."*

"Thank you, Dr. Lerma. That makes me feel better."

Leila and I continued talking about angels and she asked me what other family members or patients had reported. *"You know, Leila, for some reason, their visions always seem to appear at the corners of the room, and usually near the ceiling. It is not as unusual as you might think. In fact, Dr. Carl Jung, a famous psychiatrist who was known for his study of the* collective *uncon-*scious, *believed that children had certain sensory abilities that adults have lost."*

"Dr. Lerma, I've never had an experience like this in my whole life. There is so much we don't know about death and the afterlife. If the children are seeing her, I wish she would wake up one more time and speak to me."

Tears silently fell from her eyes, and I hugged her and said, *"She probably will, Leila. Don't lose hope."*

At that moment, we heard Joanie say, "Okay, MiMi. I'll tell her." She walked over to her mom and asked for a hug. Leila sat down on the floor, took her daughter in her arms, and gave her a warm, loving hug. Wanting to believe, Leila asked Joanie, "Were you talking to MiMi?"

"Yes, Mommy. MiMi said to tell you she loves you and not to be sad. She feels really good now and she said this hug is from her." She turned her head toward the corner of the room, "Is that right, MiMi? Did I tell it to her right?" She listened for a minute, and then she turned to look at her mother and, smiling, said, "PaPa wants you to know he loves you and is always helping all of us."

Leila started to cry uncontrollably as she hugged her daughter close. She said to me, "Joanie and Bobby Joe never met PaPa, which is what everybody called my father. He died before they were born." She looked wide-eyed at me as the tears dried up. "It's a miracle," she said quietly. "Not only did I get a goodbye from my mother, but my daddy showed up, too." She sobbed and her shoulders shook. "I missed his funeral because I got stuck in a snowstorm at an airport. I never got to say goodbye to him, but I now have my closure. I got my closure, Dr. Lerma. I need to believe this is all true." She cried on my shoulder for a few minutes, and I reassured him that her father loved her and would never want her to feel this way.

Within minutes, both children said, "Okay. Goodbye, MiMi. Goodbye, PaPa. Bye-bye, angels." Then Bobby Joe and Joanie held hands, and Bobby Joe said, "I'll take care of Mommy and Sissy like you said."

His sister sweetly kissed her little brother on the forehead, which he promptly wiped off, and she said, "I won't let him fight with anybody. I'll remind him what the angels said." Then they both walked back over to their art supplies, and sat down on the floor and started drawing pictures.

Leila said, "Dr. Lerma, I can't thank you enough for all the love and care you and your staff have provided for my mother. It's wonderful. It's a miracle. It has changed me; I'm no longer afraid of death." I told her it's what I love about my job.

I never cease to be amazed by what happens at death. It's really a magical time. As we heard MiMi's breathing pattern change, we all circled her bed and prayed the Lord's Prayer. Minutes later, she took a deep breath and whispered, "I love you, Leila." She was finally gone. It was perfect timing. Leila started crying again as I checked her mother's vital signs. I said to Leila, "You got your wish. You wished that your mother would talk to you before she died and she did. That's what I can confirm." The children looked up and waved, and then went back to sit next to their mommy. I sat down with them and told them that MiMi was gone. (In most situations such as this, family members request that I or our social worker—or both— initiate the conversation with the children, as they are so distraught and at a loss for words. This was the case with Leila.) They both said, "We know. We saw her walk into that big light with PaPa and the angels."

Doctor's Notes and More Dialogue With MiMi's Family

I'm always amazed at how well children take death. The unusual thing about this is that, younger than the age of 4, children have no concept of death. They don't really comprehend it until they're about 10 or 12, when they become abstract thinkers. I hugged the kids and asked them if the angels told them anything else that was important. Joanie showed me her drawing of a woman in front of a classroom of kids. "The angels told me when I grow up I will be a teacher for special kids, and that I will help lots of kids who need it most."

Then Bobby Joe, who was only 3, showed me a picture of what I thought was me. It was a man with a stethoscope around his neck. Flattered, I said, *"Oh, is that me?"*

He laughed. "No, it's me. I'm going to be a doctor like you. The angels said that, when you were little, they told you to be a doctor, too. They told me to tell you that."

I was shocked. At the age of 4, I had what I thought was a dream where a nice lady told me that I was going to be a doctor when I grew up. I remember thinking this dream was so real and I told my mother about it. On my following birthday, my mother gave me a stethoscope to remind me of my calling. What Bobby Joe told me fills me with joy, to this day. Then the little boy continued to surprise me even more when he said, "Oh, yes. They told me that thing around your neck is a stet-ta-cope and that I should have one to remind me that I'm going to be a doctor someday." Could this truly be happening? Was this my confirmation or was it pure coincidence? The whole situation was beyond comprehension, but compelling. A few weeks later, the family came to see me and brought some flowering plants for the garden. I gave Bobby Joe a stethoscope I had bought for him. I wanted to be sure he remembered what the angels told him, and I wanted to be his confirmation, as he had been mine.

Chapter 11

Redemption

I was having coffee with a patient's family in the hospital lounge when I got an urgent page to Room 118. It was strange how the difficult cases always appeared in this room, seemingly attracting people with complicated dying processes. This particular case involved a 53-year-old male who had been convicted of multiple murders and was being transferred to the hospice unit by the Texas Department of Corrections. George had been diagnosed with stage 4 lung cancer just months before and was in the throes of death. Handcuffed to the bed rails, I could see he was too weak to be a real threat and instructed the officers to remove them. Agreeing that he was gravely ill and too weak to be a threat, they unlocked the handcuffs and leg restraints. They left him in my care, saying, "Good luck, Doc. We hope you can get through to him. He can really be a nice guy at times."

With an officer standing guard outside his room, I began to talk to George in a comforting and reassuring manner, as I would to any patient admitted to the facility. I introduced myself and told him that I was there to help relieve his pain, anxiety, and feeling of suffocation. *"You are no longer in a prison* facility, but in a pain-management hospital unit. I know you are scared, George, but don't be. You will come to know that I am not here to judge or harass you, but to help you."

George said "I don't deserve any help. Leave me alone to die in my misery. Just leave me alone." I could hear the pain and remorse in his voice, so my heart went out to him. As a physician, my oath was to do no harm and treat everyone equally. Whatever George had done was not going to change my overall plan to bring him comfort.

Understanding the profundity of his misery, I told him I loved him as a human being and would not abandon him. Though he bellowed and threatened, the hospice team and I continued to display compassion and empathy. He calmed for a moment, telling me, "If you only knew what I did, you would understand why I act the way I do."

"Thank you for talking to me, George. You know, you are right. I have no idea what you have done and what you are feeling, but I would like to know. Conversing helps sometimes. Don't you think?"

"Yes. I know it does, but no one has ever wanted to listen when I want to talk. Not even the ministers in prison." Feeling vulnerable, George reverted back to his cantankerous and defensive ways, saying, "Stop trying to help me. Let me suffer and die in my pain."

George complained of severe pain, so I ordered parental hydromorphone. He refused the pain-relieving opiate, stating that he deserved to suffer. "George, why do you think you deserve to feel pain?" I asked.

With a glaring look, he answered, "Because I caused so much pain to others. I killed four young boys, you know. That's what I'm in jail for."

I sensed that George was challenging me to judge his past actions; nevertheless, I was disinclined, as I understood his tactics. I quickly changed the subject and asked, *"Do you believe in God?"* Mortified, he looked down and remained quiet. *"Do you believe in a loving and forgiving God?"* Still no response. *"I know you told the prison chaplain that you were raised Christian. If that's true, then you must know that His son, Jesus, died for your sins and unconditionally loves you."*

George slowly raised his head, and I noted a sense of longing for forgiveness from the God he knew as a child. He said, "That's what they keep telling me, but I'm going crazy with this guilt. I'm in agony—and not from the pain of the cancer, but from the pain of what I've done. I want to believe God has forgiven me, but my affliction is too great."

A glimmer of his humanity showed through, and I knew I had made the connection we needed. Attempting to validate his suffering, I told him that the guilt of killing four teenagers had to be unbearable. He agreed and, as I had hoped, he began to converse more honestly. I asked him, *"George, if you don't mind me asking, was it in self defense?"*

He took a long, deep breath and whispered, "It was a drug deal gone badly. I didn't even want to be there. I was a hip-hop artist in Los Angeles, and was working on a new record contract. I owed my agent a favor for the new record contract, and he took advantage of this and asked me to deliver a package. He assured me it was safe and that, if I delivered it, he would pursue more contracts. Young and eager to leave the 'hood, I agreed. That evening, we went to the rendezvous point near the beach and waited to make the exchange. We cautiously waited for the signal after the car arrived, and then proceeded to make the exchange.

"As my friend and I stepped out of our car, I carried the large foiled container and a .44 caliber pistol. As we approached each other, I saw them drawing their guns, so I quickly dropped the container, and my friend and I started shooting. We ran for cover behind my car, and within minutes there was silence and a cloud of smoke. Hearing police sirens approaching, my friend and I started running. In the end, my friend escaped, and both my record contract and I were left to rot away. That memory is so vivid for me, and it haunts me every night. I know these people were involved in the dark side of life, but I felt bad anyway. They were human beings.

"After I was diagnosed with lung cancer, I began to have visions or dreams about the four boys I killed and angels." George described a typical vision he experienced more than four weeks before, and he was still able to unveil the finest details. He talked about being visited by the four boys he murdered, who had come to forgive him. They explained to George that the key to the completion of the lesson for all involved was to attain self-forgiveness through self-love and, ultimately, by merely believing in Jesus Christ. As George enlightened me with his heartfelt life story, I could not help but see its therapeutic influence. I was in total awe.

"Dr. Lerma, one of the four boys spoke of God's love. He said that this God everyone talks about is greater than guilt.

He is more compassionate and more loving than we can fathom. The boys said, 'Look at us. We made it, and we were as sinful as you were. The spirits taught us about Jesus, and that helped us learn how to love and forgive ourselves. We all share in the God's creations with no limits including no pain, no hunger, no sadness, no poverty, and no need for money.' I know I need to accept Jesus Christ as my Lord and Savior, Dr. Lerma." He looked at me and asked what my thoughts were. Before I had a chance to reply, he said, "Never mind. It's all just a bunch of hogwash. I don't believe any of it."

"George, I believe what you have experienced. Many of my patients tell me many similar accounts about self-love and self-forgiveness as taught by angels."

"Truly, Dr. Lerma?"

"Of course, George. I would never lie to you. Why don't you tell me more about you have seen and how it is affecting you."

"I'll think about it, but I'm still feeling bad about what I did."

We spent a lot of time talking, but he could not get past his guilt. He believed he was dying and was increasingly sick because he deserved to suffer. We determined his disease came from excessive tobacco. "I started to smoke after the murders, and this would help my anxiety. Had I not killed, I may not have smoked, and subsequently may not be dying of lung cancer. I know God didn't assign this disease to me. I assigned it to myself. God tries to warn us about these dangers in the Bible, but most people don't take heed.

"I spoke to the chaplains in prison, and hoped to acquire some understanding about my visions, but that was a dead end.

They just think you're crazy. Nevertheless, I don't really blame them for feeling that way. There are a large number of psychotics." He gave up trying to find anyone to talk about his apparitions and revelations until his discussions with me and with some of the nurses.

Noticing that George was exhausted, I ended the conversation and told him to get some rest. *"I'll be back in the morning, and I would like to hear more about your life story."*

Before I left, I asked if he wanted something for pain or to sleep. For the third time, he refused, citing the same reason. I respected his decision and left. As I stepped out the door, he quietly said, "Thank you." My heart was warm all over.

The next morning, as I entered George's room along with the hospice team, he smiled and quickly told me about a vision he had early that morning. He was sure it occurred while he was awake, but he was starting to doubt himself. The social worker, the nurse, and I sat down and attentively listened to his enigmatic account. "Around three in the morning, a bright light in the room woke me. Instead of nurses, I saw two floating apparitions to the left of my bed. Feeling a bit apprehensive, I called out to the officer outside. As he walked in, the spiritual beings disappeared. Now I was sincerely frightened.

"Within minutes, they reappeared, and this time I felt more peaceful. One entity was brightly white and about 8 feet tall with flowing golden hair. The one to his left was about the same height, but just a dark silhouette. In fact, I remember that the being was darker than the darkness in the room. They appeared to be communicating and, after about five minutes, the white being turned toward me to let me know they were here to help me, and the dark being remained silent. At one point, the dark angel was coming toward me and then I saw a dark figure pop out of me. Both beings were now to the left of me and there was no sign of the beautiful, white apparition. The entire room was left an oddly bright black. They appeared to be conversing, but I couldn't hear anything. I felt an unbelievable sense of fear. What were they doing and what did they want with me? I at last cried out, 'Why don't you leave me alone?'

"Just moments later, I noticed the dense shadow move back towards me. The apparition swiftly re-entered my body, bringing with him knowledge of my family's generational sins. I witnessed this dark entity enter my great-grandfather's body after killing a human being." George said it was then that he experienced the birth of his own darkness in addition to his family's collective sins. He was feeling physical pain down to the cellular level caused by all his addictions, physical and emotional. The dark angel explained to George that darkness was not evil as we are taught; it was merely raw human energy used with negative intentions. For example, humans can choose to use nuclear energy to make an atomic bomb to kill, or use nuclear energy to traverse the universe or create electricity for survival. Either way, it's our choice (or free will) how we want to, individually or as a group, use the energy. That choice determines the consequences we have to live with individually, or as citizens of earth.

George's life decisions (how he chose to use his God-given energy), as well as his family's, allowed genetic changes to occur that maintained and carried their life's accomplishments to their offspring. George's family was evolving, as required by nature, but towards the firmly gripped negative. This negative learned behavior as a form of survival was increasingly displayed and experienced by subsequent blood relatives, so that their genes learned to create the chemicals necessary to react similarly to certain external stimulants. In other words, if drawn into an argument, the extreme negative person would respond the way his or her body and mind was taught, sometimes taking a life, whereas someone more neutral would try diplomacy. At the extreme polar opposite, a person firmly gripped with extreme positive values, against any form of violence at all times, may find him or herself in the endangered species.

Both polar opposites are incongruent with survival and evolution, because they carry the same amount of fixed potential energy, making them dangerous. Peace and love are best learned in the neutral, or fluid, state, where energy is not fixed but free to change at will. Fluidity is having the learned ability to flow up and down, and any other way along the continuum of life. On the extreme positive side, this is a person helping the world in dramatic fashion, but with an ability to reduce his or her energy level when exposed to a dire situation, thus choosing to fight his or her battle, if you will, with compromise. George said the angels discussed the vital importance of developing the skills of compromise, peacekeeping, and balance not only within yourself, but with others. This takes tremendous patience, self-love and prayer, George replied.

I asked George if the dark entity was teaching him how to release his dark and fixed energy. He spoke of a generational sin of sorts, which was at the genetic level. First, one has to acknowledge the mechanism and then decide to re-calibrate his or her thoughts first, second, third and so on, until they become a learned behavior from the neurons in the brain, down to the genetic level. If one works diligently and prays, one can hit the exponential learning curve and accomplish this in as quickly as hours or seconds. This is only possible if one draws energy from God. To do that, one has to believe in the one higher God. This is how people can be and are healed spiritually even in the last second of life.

"Dr. Lerma, I sensed that this life is about experiencing the extremes of positive and negative and everything in between, always remembering that choices such as injuring, killing, coveting, stealing, and judging come with dire consequences. This darkness held the answer to my life-long question, and I was being given the intellectual capacity to comprehend," he explained. George continued going back in time to get a better grasp of his family's and his own problems with energies, which amounted to fear, hatred, and lack of hope. He was having a difficult time freeing the fixed energy of guilt. He needed outside help, he told me: "I just don't think I have it in me, Dr. Lerma."

"George, don't worry. I will not abandon you, and I will pray for your spiritual healing," I told him.

The white angels returned and asked him what he had learned. He could not remember anything he and I had spoken of, or what he learned from the dark angels. George spoke of the angels touching his head and opening his mind to his whole life. "I remember now. I see the devil. It's the devil and he is dark and scary," George bellowed.

The angels told him, "It's not what you think. We work together. All that darkness is a side we all have. Your darkness was so dense and heavy that it took most of your body and mind and formed a dark entity. Remember, George: God is always next to you. Just talk to Him. We are here at the end of life when everything is made clear, to review and explain things to you."

George answered, "The angels know all our feelings, all our thoughts—everything that led us to the point we're at in life. They answer unanswered questions for us." I kept reassuring him of God's promise, and that He was with him.

In that moment, for some reason, George began to trust me and believe in me as a friend, and he asked me if he was going to die. I told him yes. He asked if he was going to suffocate, and I promised him he'd be asleep. He asked, "What's the hardest thing about death?" I told him that the life review was the hard part. As his heart opened, the emotional healing began. I guess he was able to change his energy to a more fluid state. It was a miraculous shift. He was now amenable to being treated. He agreed to parenteral pain medications and nebulizer treatments with morphine for his shortness of breath. He was much more peaceful.

Sadly, he was alone most of the time. No family showed up, even though the hospice employees tried to contact them and get them involved. His son was in jail and was scheduled to be released soon. George kept saying he wanted to see his son before he left, but I felt that would likely not happen. He was slipping away. His lungs were full of fluid, he had lost 80 pounds, and he was in total kidney failure. Still, he said, "I'm not ready." I've certainly been surprised by enough lingering events that I just watched and waited to see what happened.

On Christmas day I went in, and George appeared to be conversing with someone in the corner of the room, where hundreds of other patients had described seeing angels and deceased loved ones. He was saying, "Mom, I'm not worthy to go with you. You go on." I listened. George was having a conversation with his mother. She was trying to help him, but he was refusing her help. "I'm too far gone. Just go without me." He started to cry.

I tried to comfort him and asked, *"Are you okay? What's happening?"*

He told me, "My mom. My mom is here to get me." I reminded him that his mom was still alive in New Orleans. He said, "No. She said she died after Hurricane Katrina, and she's here to help me cross over." I thought he was hallucinating at that point, because people who are delirious often report seeing family members who are alive.

I asked the social worker to call and check on his mom, as he requested. Indeed, his mother had just died, and he knew it before we did. I was mystified by all this. No one had talked to him about her death, because we had not been informed yet. I went back and told George, *"You're right. Your mom has passed away."*

He said, "She won't leave me. The angels and my mom want me to forgive myself. The dark one is right next to me. It's consuming all my energy, making me feel fearful, sad, and angry, all the feelings I felt my whole life. The bright angels say to listen to it and learn from it. It is the dark side of my life trying to communicate with me. Some acts in my life were unconditional for others, but I could not sense that side of me. My dark side had absorbed it."

At our facility, I had learned that there were light angels that came to most patients, but I had never heard anyone speak of dark angels working with the light angels and deceased loved ones, all in unison. I had seen other patients who had people from the other side appearing to help them, but his mother was especially insistent. George said that his mother had light radiating from her chest, and he could see that it was God within her that was calling him. He wanted to respond, but the darkness was absorbing the light. The angels and his mother were trying really hard to help him see the light.

Then a true miracle occurred: His son, Jerome, called and said he was heading to see him. He had been released one week earlier, but he was caught up in drugs again. When he arrived at the hospice unit, George was elated. He cried and told his son to change his life, and not to follow him down this road. "Please, Son, stop selling and using drugs. Look at what that has done to me." He shared what he had been experiencing in his life review. George told his son, "You re-live everything; you feel those you hurt and those who hurt you, and the ugly feeling is overwhelming. You feel you're not worthy to be here, and fear the coming judgment." His son started crying, and you could feel the darkness and the heaviness in the room.

Jerome described a vision, from the night before, where his grandmother had appeared to him and told him to come and visit his father because he was sick. He said it felt so real that he woke up early that day and searched for his dad "Here I am, Dad. I made it and I love you. I have always loved you, Dad," he said, as tears rolled down both of their faces.

At that moment, George said the room filled with a bright white light that penetrated into his soul. He spoke of three rays of white light coming from his mother, his son, and him, which came together and made an incredible triangle of light. George said that the dark figures outside him disintegrated, and the dark figure inside him just whizzed away and dissipated. He felt he had been healed. In the middle of that, George said that several translucent blue angels went up through the ceiling, and one said, "Don't be afraid. I am the Archangel Michael. We have tried and succeeded in battling the darkness within you. Do you believe?" George said Michael showed him how spiritual beings are continuously working to protect us from ourselves. By doing this, we are able to continue to have a chance to evolve towards God.

Growing weaker, George could barely speak but was able to mention seeing a young boy who loved God and his mom and everyone again. "I'm the young boy. Wow!" He said, "We're not just healing me, but my dad, too. We are completing blood line lessons." He listened to some soundless voice and then asked for his father. "They said, 'Your father is here, but he is working on things. You have propelled your father and those you killed into the next level of love.' That is why every soul is important." He continued, "If you could have seen how many angels and how big they were and how hard they were trying to get me to love myself. If everyone could see that, it would have been a profound and lasting effect on humanity. Not just here, but in the afterworld."

Jerome, observing this miracle, said it felt as though an angel hugged him and whispered, "Never doubt God's angels. Nothing you do is so bad that it cannot be forgiven. Humans damage us so much through judgment and abuse, verbal and emotional, affecting our identity and self esteem. Work at telling people about that. We are all responsible in the end for everything. It's our responsibility to change things. More important than that are prayer, self-forgiveness, and self-love. The light destroys the darkness if we love ourselves. Through self-love we can defeat the darkness within us. Learn from your past and move forward."

He continued, "Now I understand what people see as the devil. I understand that, as much as God lives within us, there is a dark side within us and that is the extreme of our free will. We should not hate it, but embrace it, understand it, and move forward. I only had an identity with the dark side. That was so familiar to me that it was hard to let it go. It just perpetuates itself." Then, holding his father's hand, he said a prayer out loud: "Jesus, I'm not worthy to receive you. I'm sorry, and I want to change my life. Please help me."

George, much weaker, whispered and prayed: "Lord, I love you and accept you as my savior. I am ready to give my life back to you." George had a huge smile and said, "A brighter light, the Light of God disintegrated the darkness." George then became distracted. His eyes shifted, and he said, "Isn't my mom beautiful? She's wearing white clothes with inner blue garments. Her hair is flowing. She is pure light." He counted the angels in the room and said there were 14, but that there could have been more. He told his son, "Each light molecule is an angel. Some are bigger than others."

He said, "I'm ready now. I'm holding my mom's hand." George smiled and fell back on the bed. He was gone.

Doctor's Notes
and More Dialogue With George's Son, Jerome

I followed up with George's son, Jerome, who was on probation for selling drugs. He dramatically improved his life, holds a steady job, and has a healthy marriage. He is in love with his wife and God. Jerome spends most of his extra time going to high schools to talk about his experiences, about his father's death, and about what the angels have taught him. He also attends church and works with an inner-city program providing counseling for drug addicts. He still struggles with his desire for drugs on occasion, but frequent dreams of his father and the angels refill his body.

Jerome told me, "Everyone has a struggle in this life. It's a constant process of love and self-forgiveness. You'll mess up. That's part of the learning process. My dad messed up. His dad messed up, and I messed up. Now it's different. We're changing what it means to be from this family line. Everything will be different for my son, and, if I hadn't experienced what happened with my dad at his death, I would not be able to help others, as well as my family and self." Ten to 20 young gang members have left gangs as a result of Jerome's witnessing and counseling. These other ex-gang members now frequent schools and churches, and witness themselves about how God has changed their lives. Jerome says they help each other stay off drugs.

Jerome is making a difference in the world and he is carrying on his father's new legacy: a legacy of positive change through self-forgiveness, self-love, hope, and redemption.

Chapter 12

The Phone Call

I sat in Room 226 with Mary Esther. For 88 years, she was the epitome of warmth, kindness, and unconditional love. She often spoke of Jesus, her faith, and her work at Lakewood Church. She was a devout Christian and completely accepting of her approaching death. One day, as I sat holding her hand and listening to her enchanting life stories, Mary Esther unexpectedly took a turn for the worse. Her brow showed deep creases as she whispered, "I know I don't have much time left, and I'm not afraid. I have a few regrets, and I am excited to meet my Maker, but I am worried about my son, Isaac. He's having such a difficult time with my terminal illness. His faith in God is weakening, and he is very depressed. Dr. Lerma, I just can't leave him this way."

"Mary, your son will be just fine. Our bereavement team will be there to support him and even provide necessary counseling. Isaac's sadness is quite understandable and, in fact, necessary for healing to occur. Mary, you know he loves you very much."

"I know he loves me, and I know that God will find a way to help him deal with is life. Nevertheless, I'm all the family he has. I had him late in life, after I had been told I could not

have children. He was a total surprise to his father and me—
a direct gift from God. I was 44 when he was born, and now
he's 44 as I'm leaving him. My husband and I doted on him,
but my dear husband died years ago, and neither one of us
has any family left. Isaac has devoted his life to me, always
making sure I had everything I needed. He never married and
now I wish he had someone to comfort him."

"Mary, is Isaac involved with the Lakewood ministry?"

"Yes, but lately he doesn't seem to want to go. He insists
on being with me when he's not working. I'm worried that he's
angry at God for taking me away, but it's time for me to go. I'm
tired."

*"Mary, I will sit down with him tonight and listen to his con-
cerns. I will also pray with him, Mary, and will assure him that
your transition period will be peaceful."*

With tears rolling down her cheeks, Mary prayed out loud,
"My loving God, thank you for bringing me to this loving place,
and for this young doctor who you have nurtured and guided
to pray with his patients and family. Your works, Almighty God,
are so evident. Please continue your blessings on this house of
love." With tears in my eyes and my heart filled with God's
immeasurable love, I knew at that moment that this woman
was anointed by God. She spoke with such passion and fervor;
her prayers pierced your heart with pure love. She squeezed
my hand, thanked me, told me I was a good man, and then
went peacefully to sleep. I kissed her on her forehead before I
left and thought how much she reminded me of my great aunt,
"Tia Lala"—so strong, so faithful, and so caring.

When Isaac arrived that day, I invited him into the family lounge and asked him how he was doing. At first, he pretended he was just fine, as he is not a naturally expressive person. As I probed deeper, though, telling him his mother was worried about him, he broke down and cried. He told me, "I can't do this. My mother has been my whole life. We have done everything together. I never even felt that I needed another woman in my life. We have so much in common, and we just love being together. She's brilliant, spiritual, and funny—just a wonderful person. I am so blessed to have her as my mother. Now that she is dying, I feel I don't have a life. I know she is worried about my relationship with God, and so am I. I am trying to love God as she taught me, but I just can't seem to feel him without her next to me. She is the vessel that I use to have a relationship with God. How am I going to function without her?"

My mind wandered for a moment, thinking about how I would feel if I were losing my mother. I quickly gathered my compassion and held him in my arms as he cried. All words escaped me at that moment. My heart broke as I listened and felt his deep pain. *"Let's pray, Isaac,"* I said, recalling my promise to Mary Esther. So we bowed our heads in reverence to God, praying for God's love to comfort his mother, to heal his pain, and to rekindle his personal relationship with God. Feeling God's love materialize in every fiber of his being, with conviction, Isaac prayed to God that he would be given a sign that his mother had made it to heaven. He also asked God to become his vessel and teacher. The healing that was occurring was so obvious to me: Isaac did love God. He was grieving for his loss. He asked, "Dr. Lerma, you know what I just understood?"

"No, Isaac. Please tell me."

"I understand what my mother was trying to teach me with regards to God's infinite love for us. If God gave His only Son to die for our sins, what does that say about His love for us? I do love God and thank Him for my blessings and for having such a loving mother. I will give my mother closure and let her meet the Man that sent His Son to die for my sins."

Isaac had an epiphany: The more he clung to his mother, the more she would persist in suffering so that he could find peace and closure. He explained, "It's not my love that is keeping her here but, conversely, my fear of being alone. It's all about overcoming fear. Jesus knew that most humans would feel this way at the moment of a loss and taught us how to cope. As he told his mother and John to care for each other, he was also telling all souls to find a loving, spiritual connection with another soul or souls. 'Where two or more are gathered, there I am in the midst.' I understand it." I was impressed with his healing. Parts of my soul were healing along with his. It is always amazing how God affects so many lives from the life of one. "All I want now is to know that my mom made it to heaven. Do you think that's too much to ask God for?"

"Certainly not, Isaac." I recounted a few stories of other family members receiving confirmations that their loved ones were with happy and with God.

"Dr. Lerma, I guess God understands our pain and will give us what we need to be happy and at peace with death."

"Yes. It's a natural part of our life, and we all have to experience it."

Isaac continued to vacillate with his painful emotions. He figured that, if he would go first, he wouldn't have to experience the horrible pain he was facing. He blurted out, "Why couldn't I go first?" I asked Isaac if he really wanted to die first and allow his mother to feel the pain of losing her only child. He pondered and then admitted that was selfish. "I guess there is no easy way out, but there are varying levels of pain. If we have to die, then the oldest should go first, then the youngest last. Losing a child has to be the worst. I guess God chose the worse pain: to willfully lose His Son. Wow! What a loving God we have." Isaac's recurrent intuitive leaps of insight were amazing to watch. God was certainly teaching Isaac—and in an exponential manner.

This awareness seemed to calm him, giving him peace about his mother's necessary transition. He was able to visit his mother and assure her that he had found God again: "Don't worry, Mom. I love God. You taught me well. I want you to go with God when you are ready. Just keep watch over me from the other side." Unable to talk and poorly responsive now, she just smiled, giving him the affirmation he needed. Mary Esther was given her affirmation and was now able to sleep soundly for the next couple of days.

One morning, Isaac called to say that he was having car trouble and would not be able to make it see his mother until the afternoon. He was concerned about not being able to get there and made us promise to tell his mother that he would be there as soon as his car was repaired. I went in and whispered the message to Mary Esther, and instantly she opened her eyes and tried to speak. Slowly, she was able to say, "It's for the best. It's time for me to go, and I just can't leave when he's here. The angels will take me home before he arrives." I checked her vitals. She seemed to be having a surge of energy (quite common in the last minutes to hours before death). She smiled and said she wanted to sleep. I left her with a kiss on the forehead, and she quietly closed her eyes.

Before I even got to the door, I heard a deep raspy sigh that I recognized for what it was: her last breath. I turned and saw what I thought was a whish of white smoke rise from her opened mouth. I knew she was gone. I went back to her bedside and checked her pulse. There was no sign of life. I called a nurse to Room 236 to witness as I pronounced her time of death.

The nurses tried several times to reach Isaac to notify him that Mary Esther had passed on, but the telephone line was repeatedly busy. A couple hours after her death, I was at the nurses' station asking if they had reached Mary's son, and the phone rang. The caller identification showed room number 236. The nurse picked up the phone, wondering who was calling from that room. She said, "May I help you?" She thought perhaps Isaac had entered the room and she hadn't seen him. She listened for a moment and first looked confused and then frightened. She handed me the phone and shakily indicated for me to listen to the phone. As I put the receiver to my ear, I heard a lot of static and distant voice saying, "Tell my son I'm okay. Tell my son I'm okay." The phrase was repeated a few times and then the phone went dead. The nurse said, "Did you hear her? Was that Mary Esther? It sounded just like Mary Esther."

The nurse and I stared at each other for a moment, and then we both headed for Room 236. Mary Esther was still in the bed just as we had left her. I checked her and found her quite cold and dead. There was no way she could have made that phone call, and there was no one else in the room. If anyone had left the room after making the call, we would have seen him or her from the nurses' station.

About a half hour later, Isaac arrived. He appeared to have been crying. I put my arms around him and told him that his mother had passed while he was on his way. I shared her last words, and then he asked me if I had put her on the phone to talk to him. I told him no, and asked why he'd ask. "Don't think I'm crazy, but I got a phone call from my mom telling me she was okay. She wouldn't answer me. The line then went dead. When I tried calling the nurses' station, no one answered." I told him that we were trying to call him, but that we had the same problem. "I rushed over as soon as I could get here," he said. I told him that his mom had died more than an hour ago—and that we had received a similar phone call with the same message: to tell Isaac that she was okay. He explained, "When she phoned me an hour ago, I thought she was alive and we just had a bad connection. There was a lot of static, but she kept saying, 'Isaac, I am okay. I love you. Don't worry about me. I'm okay.' I thought she was calling from the hospital, so I kept trying to phone you to see what was going on with her. Has this ever happened before?" I assured him that this was the first time we had ever experienced anything like this. "Why do you think this happened with my mother?" he asked.

I said, *"This does not surprise me, seeing how God-loving your mother was. I do feel that love is the strongest force in the universe. She wanted so much for you to know that everything was okay that she was reached across the veils and found a way to let you know. Your mother was a very strong spirit; if anyone could get through, it would be her."*

Doctor's Notes

Throughout my years as a hospice physician, this is the only time I have personally experienced something so inconceivable. Was it possible that Mary Esther was communicating from another dimension? I had heard of electronic voice phenomenon (EVP) before, but was skeptical of the accounts. Was Mary Esther's message considered EVP, using electrical phone circuit to communicate? Parts of that make sense if one believes that we continue on as an electromagnetic and intelligent energy source. If we continue in that form and with intelligence, then I guess it is plausible. Well, if one believes in God, then anything is possible. After all, Isaac did pray to God to give him a sign that his mother had made it to heaven. God is awesome.

Early in Mary Esther's admission to the hospice unit, I had many profound conversations with her. She spoke of the gift that God gives all departed souls: the chance to let certain family members know that they are safe. Mary Esther believed that each of us gets to say goodbye in the way that suits us and our loved ones best. Few dying souls wait for family members to arrive before they go; in the majority of the cases, the dying decide to leave without family present. Mary Esther explained that this is so the living relatives do not experience the pain of watching them die.

Mary Esther knew it would be too hard for her son to watch her take her last breath. So, as do many souls, she waited for an opportunity when he was unable to be there. Maybe the angels even engineered his car failure to make the transition easier for him. It's certain that they had a hand in bridging the gap between heaven and earth through this miraculous telephone call.

After his mother's death, Isaac met a nice woman in his Bible study group, after witnessing his mother's love before her death. This woman was so touched by his love that she fell in love with him. One year later, they married and now have a beautiful little girl, who they named Mary Esther. She has many of the same traits as her namesake, including a way with love and prayer.

Isaac says he still gets butterflies in his stomach when the phone rings, thinking it just might be his mother again, but so far there have been no new messages.

Chapter 13

The Circle Completes Itself

Milton Lowe, a wonderful patient, had his final prayer answered only days before his death, in 2006. The story actually began 10 years earlier, in 1996. For years President George H. W. Bush and First Lady Barbara Bush have been supporters of the hospice movement. In 1996, they played an integral part in giving life to the first non-profit hospice inpatient unit in the largest medical center in the world: the Medical Center in Houston, Texas. Barbara Bush was the keynote speaker at the dedication of the Medical Center Hospice and, as she spoke of the gift of hospice this beautiful facility would provide, she recalled, with tears in her eyes, a beautiful little girl who died from cancer at the age of 3: her daughter. Understanding the deep pain associated with the loss of a child, George and Barbara Bush hoped that the hospice house would somehow allow the most difficult journey in life to be the most fulfilling.

Ten years after the dedication, and serving as the medical director of that facility, I witnessed the gift this facility was giving to a man dying of stage 4 lung cancer. From the first day I met Milton, he was full of energy and optimism. As I sat next to him I held his hand and asked him if he had any questions. He said, "No questions, but I do have a message from the people around my bed."

"A message for whom and from whom?" I asked.

"For you and all your patients, from these six beautiful glowing beings I believe are angels."

"Are they here now?"

"Yes, and they are hugging and loving both of us," Milton described. "The message is simple and about pure love. The angels want you to tell your patients and their grieving families that God is there suffering with them and getting their minds, bodies, and spirits, ready to experience His infinite, unconditional, and healing love. To literally see His love, one must be prepared physically, emotionally, interpersonally, and spiritually. The energy evoked through illness and the desire to live focuses us on our Creator. It is through His desire to live that we learn to respect our surroundings and the life it was created for: human life. We will all be given the opportunity to comprehend this final and most precious lesson before our last breath."

"Does that mean every human on earth needs to suffer to understand the gift of life?" I asked Milton.

"Dr. Lerma, just being in this body away from God is suffering. You of all people should know," Milton replied.

"I am trying to understand, Milton."

"The angels will come to you in a short time and answer all your questions. For now, just keep loving, comforting, and laughing with your patients."

I asked Milton how God was revealing His infinite love. "Well, Dr. Lerma, the angels told me that God heard my prayer last night and had manifested it in perfection."

"What was your prayer?" I asked.

"You are going to love this," he said. As I sat on his bed, he began a marvelous story of God's love. He began by telling me that, a few years after the hospice inpatient unit was dedicated, he was commissioned by the Medical Center Hospice to make a stained-glass art piece to honor the Bush family for their support of hospice through the years. The theme given for the art piece was "Kaleidoscope of Care."

It was to be presented at the annual Texas–New Mexico Hospice Conference. However, at the last moment, the president and Mrs. Bush were unable to attend. The piece stayed at the hospice facility for several years, and Milton began to wonder, sadly, if it would ever get to President Bush and his family. One day his daughter, Jan, a social worker at the hospice house, removed it from its sad perch on a file cabinet and took it home to clean it and for safekeeping.

At his request, his daughter tried unsuccessfully a number of times to get the glass to the Bush family. She even called the Bush Presidential Library and was told they could not guarantee the Bush family would actually see it. Several attempts to contact the Bush family were made for several years and, for whatever reason, the piece did not make its way to them. (There was even discussion of re-dedicating the Texas Medical Center Hospice Inpatient facility and presenting the art piece to the Bush family then, but this was never realized.)

Milton said, "I'm sure God will get the piece to them some-day. Let's not worry. I would like to discuss my recent diagno-sis to see if there is any further treatment." He began by telling me he was diagnosed with lung cancer in May 2005. Only one week later, his wife had a massive stroke while in Austin, Texas, at a World War II army reunion. While sitting at the dinner table with his entire family, his wife experienced the signs of a stroke, her speech and level of consciousness instantly affected. In the hospital, a CAT scan revealed a massive intracranial bleed, leaving her on the throes of death. With no hope for her recovery, Milton agreed to stop artificial respiration. Much to his surprise, she started to breathe normally after extubation, but nevertheless she remained unresponsive.

At that point, his daughter called me and asked me to take over her care and have her transferred back to Houston, Texas, where she had always wanted to die. I accepted care and trans-ferred her the next day with the entire family present, includ-ing Rickey, their Boston terrier. She was immediately made comfortable and, just 24 hours later, on Mother's Day, she made her final transition back to the arms of Jesus.

Needless to say, the entire family was unable to grieve openly, as their father was quite ill with his cancer. During the following days and weeks, Milton continued his chemotherapy and radiation concurrently. Meanwhile, he found it comfort-ing to go through his wife's belongings, including hundreds of her pictures and letters. This gave him strength to endure his aggressive chemotherapy. To keep himself occupied, he began working on new stained-glass projects. One day, while setting up his work area, he came across the art piece he had made for the Bush family almost 10 years earlier. Out loud, he wondered if anything would ever happen to it—if it would ever arrive at its rightful home. Was this a metaphor? Was he really talking about his journey back to his Creator, with his wife at his side? In a silent prayer, knowing that God was coming for him soon, Milton told me that he asked his Creator to make sure the Bushes' art piece got the honor it deserved before his death. I could tell how much it meant to him. He said it would be a "ray of hope for those who would come to understand its meaning."

A few months after that, his daughter, Jan, and her husband were invited to a private screening of the new movie about Pocahontas. It was to benefit Bo's Place, a children's hospice in Houston, Texas, established after the death of Bo Neuhaus. The event was invitation-only, and Barbara Bush would be attending. "Could this be the answer to my prayer?" he wondered.

When his daughter arrived at the theater, she learned that this was an especially small group, and felt honored to be a part of the event. While standing in the lobby, she turned around, and Barbara Bush was standing next to her. Milton said his daughter was surprised, to say the least, and it was one of the few times she found herself speechless. Recognizing the rare opportunity, she gathered her confidence and began to talk to her. Jan introduced herself as someone she "didn't know from Adam's housecat." The First Lady smiled and said she didn't know anyone there. Jan went on to say she had something that belonged to her but didn't know how to get it to her. Mrs. Bush seemed amused and suggested that Jan not try to bring it to her house, as she might be shot. Jan assured her she did not want to be shot, and then explained what the item was with a brief history. As she heard Jan tell her the story and that her father, dying from cancer, would be so happy if the stained-glass piece found its rightful home before he died, a tear rolled down her cheek. Barbara Bush immediately suggested that Jan contact her secretary to make arrangements for her to receive the piece. "This was definitely more than a coincidence; it was a Godsend," Milton explained.

The next day, Jan called Barbara Bush's office and spoke with her secretary. She was aware of the conversation and asked when it could be delivered, as she would have to get Secret Service clearance. Jan suggested a day, and the secretary concurred. Milton was so excited and full of joy when he heard of the conversation and plan. Though he was weak, he was strong enough to supervise the cleaning of the piece, and Jan made sure it met with his approval.

Milton looked so happy, even though he had been quite sick. Jan delivered the piece to the office as scheduled and spoke to the Secret Service people, who then called Mrs. Bush's secretary. She eloquently expressed appreciation for it and assured Jan that the president and Mrs. Bush would see it. When Milton heard the piece had been delivered, he breathed a sigh of relief and said, "Finally." He said his daughter and he felt such a sense of completion and commented that the angels told him that this was exactly the way God planned it.

A few days later, Jan daughter received a lovely note from President and Mrs. Bush.

January 26, 2006

Dear Jan Taylor,

The absolutely beautiful art glass circle that your dad made for George and me ten years ago arrived here (our home) yesterday. I am overwhelmed and I do hope you will tell your dad just how thrilled we are with it. It is stunning, and after much debate, we are sending it to George's library in College Station where it will be seen by thousands over the years.

We are very proud of hospice and especially the Medical Center Hospice. It has become such an important part of our medical center and has grown across the country.

I thought the evening for Bo's Place was wonderful. I will confess I admire Bo's Place much more than the movie. I thought the movie was only fair. Do go see "Glory Road." It is a great movie. Hug your Dad.

Warmly,

Barbara Bush

Only days later, I admitted Milton into our inpatient hospice facility—the facility that the Bushes helped fund. During the last days of his life, as most terminally ill patients do, Milton began to see angels, including his deceased relatives, and his wife, his beautiful friend and lover. He said that the angels were telling him about how God heard his prayer and initiated a course of events that would see that he would attain a comforting closure to his life. He was told that God would answer those prayers that are not selfish and that ultimately glorify His name.

He went on to say that the angels told him that it is through unconditional love, selflessness, and joyful suffering that miracles occur. His wife told him that events transpired this way in order to touch and comfort those with open hearts.

Two days later, Milton died, almost on the anniversary of his wife's death. With his daughter and the chaplain in the room, Milton smiled and reached upward with his hands as he took his last breath. Jan and the chaplain stated that, as he exhaled his last breath, a white flash emanated from his chest and flew out the window. Several hours after this, people who walked into his room were able to experience the remnant static energy.

Milton was truly joyous as he died, and his long and difficult journey had been willfully and successfully completed. I couldn't help but wonder if Bo Neuhaus, for whom the benefit was when Jan and Mrs. Bush finally connected, had anything to do with the completion of the circle. Either way, a prayer was answered and the circle of life was completed.

Chapter 14

The True Believer

Dr. Johnson was a fascinating man. He was highly intelligent; a dedicated doctor, lawyer, and judge; and a noted atheist. I knew of him prior to his arrival at hospice, as his illustrious reputation preceded him. At age 68 and dying of lymphoma, he was transferred to our hospice inpatient unit for pain control and terminal care. He was a gentle and selfless man who was born as an only child and became an orphan at age 8 when his parents perished in a car accident. I was honored to have spent one wonderful week becoming acquainted with him and learning a great deal about his beliefs, life choices, and experiences at the end of life.

He began his career as an emergency room physician in a Lutheran hospital. He was raised Lutheran, and he grew up loving the church and wanted to be of service. That's why he became a doctor. He also liked the high level of intensity of the emergency room, as working there challenged both his medical skill and fast-thinking mind. However, after a couple of years, he began to question his choice, as he had seen so many horrible things, among them two children who had been so brutally abused by their parents that they died from the injuries, several young children who were innocent bystanders killed by drive-by gunshots, and a child whose hand was cut off by his father for knocking over his beer.

Dr. Johnson could not believe the terrible things that people were doing to each other—and especially to their children. His own parents were killed by a drunk driver, and it hurt him so deeply that all he could think about was how to stop the seemingly unnecessary acts of violence through stricter laws and increased social awareness. As a result of watching so much suffering, pain, and violence, Dr. Johnson declared that there could be no God, because a benevolent God would never allow such atrocities to occur. He decided that, if there were no God to intervene in the chaos, he would have to do something himself. First, because of his parents' death, he got involved with Mothers Against Drunk Driving (MADD), and then he helped found Teens Against Drunk Driving. Still he felt it was not enough.

After a great deal of soul-searching regarding what he could do to help prevent family violence, instead of just patching up the harm that had already been done, Dr. Johnson decided to run for city council. He did not win, but he developed many powerful friends, and his passion to stop the violence grew even stronger. He went back to school, earned his law degree, and became a family practice attorney. Driven by his anger and personal grief, he exceedingly strove to make a difference. During his career, he introduced a variety of legislation that has resulted in more watchfulness of abusers, more significant levels of punishment, and more available and mandated family counseling. Dr.Johnson said that, since he decided there was no God, his personal sense of responsibility had increased. It was up to him and to each of us to make a difference in our world. No one else is going to do it for us.

I asked him if he really didn't believe in God. He said that, as he lay on his deathbed, he wondered about that, too. He said, "We all take out insurance polices, and I had one in place for the afterlife as a child, but then I gave it up because of the horrible things I saw: man's inhumanity to man. But," he continued, "in the last few days, I've been seeing and experiencing things that seem beyond my control and outside my belief system. I am looking at life from a new perspective."

He asked me if he was hallucinating and if people really see things when they're dying. I told him, *"People see things similar to what you're seeing all the time. All kinds of people— murderers, child molesters, probably even that guy who chopped off his child's hand—claim to see comforting apparitions. What do yours look like?"*

He confided, "They are bright white and very comforting. They entice me to see myself for who I truly am. I don't feel deserving of their comfort because I abandoned my faith and denied God."

Trying to comfort him, I continued to share stories of other patients who felt the way he did and ultimately found peace: *"I feel that the angels come for everyone no matter what their life has been. The love that comes from the angels restores us, no matter what our beliefs are."*

He asked, "How does that happen?" I advised him to ask the angels, but he said, "They don't talk to me." I told him to just about think his questions, and that the answers would come to him in sort of extrasensory phenomenon (ESP) form. He laughed and said that he would try that as an experiment, although he didn't really believe in ESP. He was truly a wonderful man, even though, as an atheist, people judged him and told him he was going to hell. He hated hypocrisy, and he hated that people went to church, declared their faith, and then really didn't care about all the terrible things happening around them. I asked if he was spiritual. He said, "Yes. I think so. It is my spirit that detests what I see here. That spirit has led me to try and make a difference."

I told him, *"God loves you, and you've done a great job, and there's nothing to feel bad about."* I told him that I've cared for a few atheists and they are usually highly intelligent, caring people, and they all see the angels at the end of their lives. I presume that, because of the life they led, belief wasn't really necessary. Although, when they see the angels, their belief usually shifts toward the acceptance of a higher power.

Dr. Johnson still had a hard time accepting as true the mystical experiences surrounding him, especially with his extreme adherence to logic. Taking his logic into consideration, I began to converse in terms of physics. Because he was a doctor, I was speaking his language. He asked, "Do you think I'm going anywhere after I die, or do we just cease?"

I told him, *"All I know is what physics say: Energy cannot be created or destroyed; it only changes form."* Humans are highly electromagnetic beings, one of the strongest self-contained and intelligent forms of energy on the plant. We have enough electricity to power certain equipment in our homes. I told Dr. Johnson, *"You or your spirit will never die. Only your body will change form.*" He understood that concept, and he started thinking about it and coming to a greater understanding as we discussed it further.

Dr. Johnson cocked his head and asked, "Have you ever seen anything?"

"No, but there have been reports of spheres of light radiating from patients' solar plexus."

"Are they always spherical?"

"Sometimes they're wavy or slightly distorted, sort of globular, but usually they are round."

"That's funny. Why do you think they exude light?"

I thought about it and remembered, *"If you let energy follow its natural flow, it will almost always form a sphere because of gravitational forces. It naturally becomes spherical in shape, like the planets."*

"That's right. Why does it have to be different? Why do we have to make it something so different? Probably it's all perfect as it is and not as strange as we think it is."

I told him that some people have said that, when we leave, heaven is the same as earth, but it is a perfected place. As we continued to talk over the next few days, Dr. Johnson looked a lot more peaceful, and resolved his own beliefs and came to grips with his strange experiences.

He saw that his mom and dad had entered his room one evening, and he just couldn't believe it. He questioned the amount of morphine being administered. (It was not a dosage that would cause hallucinations.) He went on to describe what his eyes and brain envisioned. "When my parents entered my room, they had a stranger with them. They introduced him as the drunk driver who had killed them. They wanted me to know that it all worked out the way it was supposed to. I asked my parents, 'If it worked out to perfection, then why did it pull me away from God?' They told me that it needed to be as it was to make me follow my path.

"I asked them, 'Don't you think I would have done these things anyway?' and they said, 'No. You were getting depressed and jaded and close to quitting before you embarked on your mission.'"

Although Dr. Johnson still felt it could have been done in an easier fashion, he understood what they were telling him and accepted that there was some truth in it. He said he understood it all at that point, but he couldn't really explain it to me. "You would have to see the thoughts the way the angels showed it to me. It was light years ahead, pre-events, past, present, and future—all intermingled—and it's so massive, it's impossible to understand unless they show it to you."

He said that it resonated through him and took over every cell in his body. Knowing that God is always with us, and the comprehension of His part in the drama, kept growing and growing and growing. He looked at me and said, "Don't worry, and don't let anyone pull you away from your passion. Every soul can help the world if it's done in pure passion and with unconditional love for others. And, what you do for them is wonderful as well. It's all mutually rewarding. It's for your own heart, too." I was really moved by what he said and have never forgotten the words and the feeling behind them.

The next day Dr. Johnson said, "My time has come, and I'm ready." Within hours, he died peacefully, holding my hand and saying, "Thank you."

Doctor's Notes
and More Dialogue With Dr. Johnson

People always ask me if atheists have horrific deaths. I tell them that, from my experience, they have easier deaths than most. Dr. Johnson said that Paul came to him and explained who he was and what a great passion he had for what he believed. Paul wrote much of the New Testament with the same passion. Paul said, "Look at who I am, what I did, and how I became a vessel for God's glorious plan. He used you in the same way. He worked through your anger and passion."

Desiring to know more about his spiritual experiences, I asked Dr. Johnson to expand on happiness, suffering, and diseases. He said that, in terms of joy, when we die and we finally move beyond the angels, we come face to face with our Creator. By that point, we've been reviewing our lives constantly with the angels and our deceased loved ones. When God steps in, all angels help you focus on our Creator. "Our thoughts and wrongdoing are not a big part of the conversation with God. Our conscience takes care of that. However, during the review process, we never ask ourselves what we did to have fun. God asks us what we did to make ourselves happy on earth, because it's through true joy fueled by truth and love that we can make more changes than through anything else."

I asked, *"If happiness is that important to God, how can we be joyous when people are suffering and hurting, including ourselves?"*

He said, "To understand this, one must understand the creation of free will. God's most important gift to us was free will. Through our free will, we can choose happiness instead of suffering. Joy is at the core of everything. It is the final outcome of everything we do. For some it might be working with orphans or abused children—or for you, Dr. Lerma, it is working with dying patients. Although it may be difficult to do some of this work, the key element is your joy and passion. All our passion is converted into joy. Joy is God's currency." Dr. Johnson understood that he sought his passion even though it was activated by anger. He recognized that he had his joy all along, through his passion to help others.

Some of us deny our passion, even though it's set in the beginning of our life. That happened to me. I had an incredible conflict within. Of course, healing occurred when I finally accepted and loved my entire being; a being filled with weaknesses and strengths. Dr. Johnson reminded me, "Helping others is what drives you and me. It's not the money or the place you live, but what's stored inside your heart and soul. Everything stored there carries into the afterlife." He told me that he saw all the children he had helped in the emergency room, even the ones who had died, and that they were grateful to him for his efforts and his compassion. He said, "You can change things through joy and happiness. This is the time to move away from suffering and to embrace our joy and passion."

He also told me, "If you choose to follow your passion in life, you do get to share your gifts with the world. Don't be concerned about other people's suffering so much that you take away their opportunity for growth." He understood that, as we gain further education and understanding, there comes a point where you don't have to go through lessons anymore. He said, "Dr. Lerma, someone can just tell you about his or her experience or outline the consequence of taking an action, and you can get it and choose not to go through the pain. But that only happens as we evolve."

He cautioned me, "You have to be very careful who you take pain from. Be careful about what you let into your life. Not everyone has the ultimate truth and understanding." He said, "There is no doubt that darkness exists, so don't get drawn in. Let other people learn their lessons, and you learn your own lessons. If you fall down, get up and go again. Suffering teaches you when to trust other people as they share their lessons. It develops your discernment."

It was a lot to take in, but the message was very similar to other messages the angels have brought through Buddhists, Christians, Hindus, and now an atheist. In the end, Dr. Johnson was one of the truest believers I've ever met. His acceptance of God's very existence as well as that of the angels was truly profound. Love is the truth of God for everyone, no matter what you believe, and no matter how you live your life.

Chapter 15

A Test of Faith

I t was mid-spring, and I was sitting on an old wooden bench nestled within the trees of our facilities garden. Rabbi Levine was next to me discussing a patient who was to be admitted later that day. Rachel, 48 years old and four weeks from death, was both awe-inspiring and enlightening. By the time of Rachel's death, her Rabbi and I came to believe, without a question in our minds, that she was a highly evolved spirit.

Rachel came to the Houston Medical Center from Argentina, with the hope of finding an experimental drug that would halt her disease progression. Her family thought she suffered from a Parkinson's-like disorder, but Rachel was a victim of Huntington's chorea, an autosomal-dominant disorder. She was diagnosed at age of 36, in the prime of her life. Rachael and her husband, Benjamin, had two sons in their 20s, which was the other tragedy of the situation, as Huntington's chorea usually afflicts 50 percent of siblings within a family. The terrible fate that awaited one of these young men was inescapably horrifying. We discovered that Rachel's mother had Huntington's chorea, too, but it was never diagnosed.

This progressive and fatal disease affects the basal ganglia in the brain, which increases dopamine, an excitatory neurotransmitter that causes involuntary writhing muscular movements, leaving patients unable to care for themselves. Their cognitive function is maintained for years, only for them to succumb to the ravages of dementia just prior to death. Some people confuse Huntington's chorea with cerebral palsy or Parkinson's. (Parkinson's is actually its direct polar opposite: a disease lacking in dopamine.) The fact that dementia doesn't make its presentation until a few years before death makes it even more cruel and difficult for patients to deal with their physical decline. As the disease progresses, patients lose their ability to walk, talk, swallow, and, less often, breathe. In Rachel's case, she developed respiratory dysfunction as she suffered from severe emphysema from the use of tobacco. In the end, it is usually aspiration pneumonia, cardiac problems, and, more often than not, suicide. It is a cruel, tragic, and heartrending disease.

Currently, genetic testing can be performed to determine if one will develop Huntington's chorea, and one day hopefully there will be a way to prevent it. Rachel's two sons were both informed about this testing, which put a tremendous stress on them. They were torn between wanting to know and being afraid to know which one would develop the disease. The boys were absolutely traumatized by their mother's diagnosis and then had the added news of the 50 percent probability of one of them also getting the disease. By the time I met Rachel, her boys were so distressed that they chose not to watch their mother endure the harsh process of dying with this disease.

This caused a great deal of sorrow for Rachel, though she tried to be strong and say she understood. Benjamin, Rachel's devoted husband, however, hardly ever left her side.

Because of a tracheotomy, Rachel could not speak. She suffered from uncontrolled body spasms and was being fed intravenously. Her most urgent desire was to speak, which meant weaning her from the mechanical ventilator and then removing the tracheotomy tube. Because I felt that death was near, further aggressive treatments were futile, and there was no hope of recovery, I honored her request. We changed over to a high-powered non-invasive ventilator. The small breathing tube that fit tightly to the nares was connected to a highly advanced computer that delivered a forced amount of oxygen through her nose instead of her tracheotomy. We were able to remove the endotracheal tube, thus allowing her to talk. This was the first time she had spoken in almost six months. This was so exciting for her and Benjamin, who wanted to hear her voice one more time before she passed on. Surprisingly, once Rachel was off her previous treatment modalities, she actually improved.

The day after we removed the endotracheal tube, Rachel woke up and, unbelievably, began to converse with her family. Her voice was hoarse and raspy, but understandable. For Rachel, it was a miracle. By the end of the third day, I walked in with a colleague and a nurse, planning to examine Rachel and obtain blood gases to assess her status. However, there were over seven people in the room, including Benjamin, visiting Rachel. I finished going over Rachel's chart and said, *"Y'all go ahead and visit. I'll come back later."*

As I turned to walk away, I heard a forceful voice say, "NO! I have a message for you!" I whirled around to face the voice, and everyone in the room was staring at Rachel in stunned disbelief. Her voice was stronger than it could possibly have been. I'm sure my eyes were bugging out of my head.

"A message for who?" one of the friends asked.

"Him," Rachel replied.

I pointed to myself as I asked in surprise, *"For me?"*

"Yes! You! I have a message for you," Rachel insisted.

"From whom?" I asked. Because I've witnessed hundreds if not thousands of angelic or spiritual visitations during the death process of my patients, I was well oriented to such scenes, but seldom have the spiritual visitors come to give a message to me. Frankly, I was more than surprised.

"The message is from Jesus."

Now I was really shocked. *"Jesus? I thought you were Jewish."*

"I am."

"Is it really from Jesus?"

"Absolutely," she insisted.

Benjamin, astounded, asked her what she was talking about. She explained to him that this was not a hallucination or from the medications. This was as real as she was seeing Him. "Then, where is He?" Benjamin asked.

"At the foot of the bed." She pointed, as if we should be able to see Him, too. I remembered that hundreds of other patients had seen angels to the side of them or in the corner of the room. I only remembered a handful, though, who had claimed to see Jesus, and they saw Him at the foot of the bed, as Rachel claimed she had. I always wondered what the reason for the choice in locations was. This was fascinating to me.

Rachel turned away from her husband and toward me, and she asked if I had prayed for something special the night before.

"*Yes,*" I said, hesitant to share personal information with a patient.

"It's about your son, Mark, isn't it?"

I was stunned. I had never mentioned my children's names, but I am divorced and, just the day before, had discovered the disturbing fact that my children were in an abusive situation. My hands were tied, and my children were not being properly protected. I had been praying with all my heart for my children's safety and for a solution to this problem.

"Jesus heard your prayer, and He says to tell you that it will be okay. He is watching over you and your children. He wants you to stay here where you are and to continue to impart the information about what you're doing in hospice. He doesn't want you to move back home," she said. I was flabbergasted and speechless. Rachel repeated emphatically, "He wants you to stay here and share everything you're learning." The people in the room were staring at me now.

"Have you met this doctor before your visit to the hospice?" one of her friends asked.

"No," Rachel replied, and then looked back at me. "Horrible, disturbing things may occur in your life. But always understand that that He is the one who guides your life and protects you. It's all in his control."

"*I understand,*" I replied, though I didn't like the dire sound of her warning. Who wants to hear that horrible things are going to happen?

Rachel continued, "He wants to prove the truth of this information to you more fully," she said, as she turned to the nurse. "You have a son named John, don't you?"

"Yes," the nurse replied quietly, looking down at her feet, not too happy to be the subject of this public scrutiny.

"You had him by C-section, didn't you?" Rachel continued, "Then he was molested and died."

"Oh, my God," the nurse said, and she started crying.

Everyone in the room was cast into a fascinated and horrified silence. Rachel ignored them all. "It's right, isn't it?" she asked the nurse.

"Yes. All of it's true."

"Well, Jesus wants to tell you your son is here with Him now. Jesus is at the foot of my bed and He wants you not to worry. Your son is fine now." The nurse couldn't speak, but nodded her understanding. The other doctor with me was a student, and she was totally unprepared for all this. She'd never witnessed anything like it in her entire life. In fact, none of us had. It shook her medical mind to its core.

Looking around the room at Rachel's friends from her synagogue, I could feel and see that they were also being rocked to their core. They didn't want to believe anything they were hearing, yet their hearts could feel the truth seeping in. A few of them were visibly angry, which is a primordial reaction to fear. Rachel saw their anger, looked one of her friends in the eye, and said, "Jesus wants to tell you to re-evaluate your faith. He asked me to tell you that I have been seeing Him for a long time. He said not to forget that He was born Jewish."

"What are you saying?" Benjamin asked.

Rachel answered, "Jesus asked the same thing of me, and I chose to follow Him as the Son of God."

"Why didn't you tell me?" he asked.

"Because I couldn't talk with a ventilator hose thrust down my throat. That's why I asked to have it removed. He told me I had to tell people all this." Benjamin hung his head. He couldn't look at her at that moment. I could tell he was overwhelmed by everything he had been hearing. Rachel continued, "Jesus has appeared to me often. He told me exactly why we are Jewish as well as the chosen people. Politics was intimately involved in the conception of this astounding defining moment. Evil loves politics. Remember the Pharisees, Benjamin? Well, that one move against him two thousand years ago was political. There was nothing spiritual about it. It's still about politics. It's not about religion."

Benjamin was really upset. He was sure that Rachel was hallucinating, and he blamed me. He demanded, "What are you giving her? What kind of medicine could make her hallucinate this way?"

I responded gently, realizing his distress, saying, "*Truthfully, sir, this is the first time she's been able to talk, and she's not on any medications that are sedating.*"

Rachel spoke again. "Jesus wants you to listen to His words and you will know the truth. He came to teach us. This is real, Benjamin."

I reflected for a moment and asked Rachel, *"Can I ask a question of Jesus?"*

"Ask it."

"A few of my patients have seen Jesus, even non-Christians, but not one has been Buddha or Muhammad. Why is that?"

"That's not important," Rachel gently chastised me.

"Okay, then. One more question. Why is he always at the foot of the bed?"

She smiled. "Don't you know? He's kneeling down in total love and humility and washing my feet. You see, Dr. Lerma, He does this for several reasons, but the only one I am allowed to reveal is the most important one."

Eagerly, I asked her to tell me. She went on to say that it is about unconditional love and humility. "God wants us to know that He understands that this world is tough and that it will make sense to all of us one day."

"Very tough," I agreed.

Rachel continued, "I asked Him about my disease, you know."

"You did? What did He tell you?" I asked, always eager for information on a patient's illness.

"He said that subconsciously there is another life going on. We get very close to that life, that spiritual connection, through illness. Illness brings us close to God. First we get angry, then we deny, and ultimately we attempt acceptance. We accept God and his will. There is something greater in our lives always going on. Actually, we are always communicating with God about our life, but on a subconscious level. That's why we have to pull away from our human mind." Rachel paused for a moment and then brightened. "Oh, yes! I remember now! I had forgotten. But now I remember that I accepted this challenging disease for a reason, and I would do it over again."

Rachel exclaimed, "Yes, I would, and I would do it because of how close it has gotten me to Jesus. I know my dark side and my good side. Everything we do is to help the world. All my pain and suffering is to raise the level of humanity. All my sacrifices go toward making God's creation a better place for our children and grandchildren and all the generations to come."

"This is unbelievable," Benjamin said.

I was thinking to myself that this was precisely what my Catholic religion taught me.

Rachel went on: "God gives you the choice to die, or to suffer and experience the pain. It's up to you. God does not play games. We operate under faith for a reason. We are trying to move toward God and understand the craziness in the world, like murders and illness and war. These things are our human creations, and they all stem from fear, judgment, and guilt. Now we're trying to gravitate away from that hurt and suffering into an easier way of life."

I left Rachel that day with a million thoughts in my head. Every time I have one of these encounters with a dying patient, I think I've heard it all, and then there is someone who sheds even more light on this human experience, just as Rachel did. I remembered an interview with Pope John Paul II. When asked about his illnesses, including Parkinson's, he said that, if he had to do it over again, he would still choose to suffer his illnesses because their exigent qualities bring about eternal healing by bringing us closer to God. He had said exactly what Rachel was saying.

A few days later, we had our next encounter. Rachel was lucid and very talkative again. This seemed impossible from a medical point of view, but it was happening. I listened and learned. "I also know you have an illness you are going through now, though you are doing better since you gave it up to him. There is a time in everyone's disease when you see it as a benefit, and are relieved from its depressive effects. It takes a while to get there."

"Yes, it does, Rachel, but it has given me great compassion for my patients."

"You're where I am," Rachel commented. "That's why you do what you do. Do you understand what I'm saying?"

"I think so," I replied.

"It's about helping yourself first, then helping others." She continued, "My disease made me love myself more. Those who are angry all the time can't be helped. That is their free will. Those people choose the familiarity of anger and control. Those who are poverty-stricken or victims of war cannot find it in themselves, and they are being helped by us."

"That's comforting to know," I said.

"But, you don't have to have a disease to help others. Just being in this body and getting up every day helps others as long as we find some joy in it and perform random acts of kindness.

You see those bumper stickers around. Well, that works miracles. The Angels told me to read from 2 Corinthians 5:6: 'While we are in the body, we are separate from the Lord.'

"So, just being in the body is painful because what we really want is to be close to God. Suffering, in its true form, is to be separated from God. You wake up to negativity each day. People have to struggle so hard to find the positive in life."

"Buddhists try to dissect their thought processes. They try to become positive. It's through being positive that healing occurs," I said.

"Are you talking about healing the body?" Rachel asked.

"Yes," I answered.

She continued, "But that's also a problem with people. They want to heal their body when they need to heal their relationship with God."

I asked her, *"How can we use this to help others?"*

Rachel seemed to listen for a moment to an unseen being before answering, "Once a person has the understanding I have been given, then God can heal us. But we have the choice. Most people who get this level of understanding actually decide they don't want to be healed. They want to help people. It's an act of unconditional love."

I continued to muse, *"I've always heard that the Bible says, 'When your time is up, it's up.'"*

She replied, "God can extend your time if you choose to be healed. The only reason He will do that is if you use that extra time to do something unconditional for others with an ultimately positive outcome for humanity." She smiled and went on to say, "You see, it's about helping ourselves first, and then we can help others. We have to be charitable and compassionate to ourselves. It's okay to love ourselves.

"What we do for ourselves helps everyone else. Take some time away to be by yourself. We should all be finding the joy in this world and joy in God. There is so much in this world to see. Go see it. Observe the world and get to know its entire people."

I considered what she was sharing with me and how it applied to my life. "You know what one of the biggest lessons in the 20th century is?" she continued.

"No, I have no idea what that could be," I said, eager to hear her next revelation.

"To forgive Hitler."

"What? You were told that?" I reflected on her statement in complete surprise. That was a big test of faith for a Jewish woman.

"Yes. You see, even Hitler, who was loved by God, was a product of a colossal evil act. He was born of a German woman, who loved him very much. His biological father? A Jewish man she worked for and who raped her repeatedly. Hitler's darkness was nurtured and perpetuated by horrific physical and emotional abuse. At one point, he was hit so hard that he slipped into a coma for several days. That generational sin was massive. If you are capable of understanding that he confirmed man's potential for darkness and cruelty, then the knowledge that we are not that different will allow us to choose external and internal forgiveness. This will secure our path towards an all-loving and all-forgiving God.

"Those who are willing to stay here and take care of others and suffer separation from God, which is very painful, are the beloved of God. God only allows us to suffer for a limited time, though."

"*Really?*" I was amazed by everything I was hearing, and some of it I had considered many times.

"That's important for everyone to remember," Rachel said.

We ended our discussion, as Rachel was growing weaker. During the next few days, several uncanny and fascinating things began to happen to Benjamin. I was in Rachel's room when Benjamin spoke of his recent experiences. "Dr. Lerma, I feel compelled to tell you that I, too, have begun having dreams or perhaps visitations from Jesus." This time it was my turn to be blown away. Benjamin had been so angry when Rachel first spoke about Jesus that I didn't think I would ever hear what he was about to tell me.

"I've had these far-fetched dreams. Jesus spoke to me. Rachel came into my bedroom and spoke to me, too. I was flying around with angels, and I have never even believed in angels. All of them were trying to get me to understand what Rachel has been saying. She told me I had to forgive Hitler. I was told that I had to love everybody—not just my family and friends, but everyone in the world, especially my enemies and myself."

"*Amazing,*" I replied, as Benjamin pushed on before he lost his nerve.

"I was told that sometimes we have to die earlier than expected. Dying as victims of murder, war, home violence, circulating man-made toxins, such as in cigarettes and even capital punishment, is not part of God's plan. With each killing, we plant the seeds of more hatred. God is calling us now to stop killing. I was told we should stand back the way Gandhi did. It's time for peace."

"You were told that?"

"Yes. In my dream," Benjamin said.

"It was no dream," Rachel interjected. "It really happened. I was there."

"Well, it did seem pretty real," Benjamin admitted. "They said if we really stood back like Gandhi, God would protect us. He loves all of us." Benjamin paused abruptly. He looked at me very intensely. "In my dream, Rachel told me, 'Do not worry. Even if you don't believe, you're riding on my belief.'" That sounded reminiscent of something I had heard before.

One of the very last things Rachel told me concerned Muslims: "I want you to know what I was told so you can share it. There is something called generational sin. It all started back with Abraham, Ishmael, and Isaac. It was all about pride and lack of faith. Abraham was Jewish. If he had accepted his responsibility for the child he bore with his servant, God would never have divided the land. We are the chosen people to restore that peace; anyone who believes in the Jew of Nazareth as the Son of God is Jewish and chosen. We have been chosen to repair our forefathers' mistakes. It's our responsibility. It's all of us together, working for peace."

Later that evening, Rachel died peacefully.

Doctor's Notes and More Dialogue With Rachel's Husband, Benjamin

Over the last two weeks of Rachel's life, Benjamin stayed by her side. She lived for four weeks off the ventilator, which far exceeded the expected two days. It was during the last week of Rachel's life that she spoke of Jesus. Eventually, her disease advanced to the point where she slipped into a coma. That's when I knew that death was very close.

During those last days I got to know Benjamin quite well. All he had left were the dreams of Rachel and God. He had to rely on those dreams and faith. Knowing and believing that her spirit survives brought him great comfort. I shared my stories of other patients with him to help him through his uncertainties and grief.

Benjamin shared the following: "There was something in my soul, and my gut that told me all along that something in my Jewish faith was not being tapped. It wasn't anyone's fault. I just didn't know what it was. I love my wife so much and, because of her, I'm growing in my love for Christ as my true Rabbi."

One of the last things Benjamin said to Rachel was: "Honey, thank you for helping me understand the truth about Jesus. This gave me back my faith and will to live. I believe in my heart I should be a Messianic Jew now. It's not an easy road. I plan to move to Israel, with God's help, and do what I can to spread the truth of Jesus. I know I'm just one guy, but you've taught me that all your suffering has made a difference. Maybe I can make a difference, too."

When Rachel died, it was interesting to me that all of her family finally came together in love. The bitterness that had kept her sons away had dissipated. Because of the truth of her messages to me about my life, I can only believe that the angels, Jesus, and those she was hearing from the heavenly side of our existence delivered all of Rachel's messages. I feel a responsibility to share her messages with everyone who can read these words.

These profound moments that I share with my dying patients are more than precious to me. I feel that listening to them and relating the information they are receiving is vital to the earth at this moment in human history. I am only one man, one doctor, but, as Benjamin said, I will not turn a deaf ear nor a blind eye to what is happening in my presence.

Rachel's divine prophecy has allowed many of my staff to strengthen their faith, and this includes me. During those last four weeks of Rachel's life, I knew medically that she should have died almost immediately after her respirator was removed. She remained alive during that time for an important reason. Rachel appeared to be driven by a special kind of energy, intention, and purpose. She was suffering to raise the consciousness of humanity.

She wanted desperately to share these profound spiritual messages with her husband, her family, and me. I am so very delighted to report that she accomplished all that she meant to do, and I am committed to sharing her story to my patients, their families, and the world. She was certainly a woman I will never forget.

Surely, Rachel now has great comfort in knowing, even on the other side, that she left the world a better place because of the life she lived. As I continue my work in hospice, I pledge to all who read these stories that I will listen, take notes, and remember everything that is told to me. To the best of my ability, I have clearly expressed Rachel's messages and the intent of the beings that are speaking directly to all of us. I also try to listen to my own heart and the messages that come to me, and share them as well. No one has to die to see angels. They are here for us when we are here for them.

Chapter 16

The S Factor: The Supreme Act of Love

A s I walked along the vast network of passageways within the hospital on my way to see my next patient, I passed the neonatal unit and heard the cry of a newborn baby. My mind wandered for a moment, and I began to wonder about the origin of life and its plan. I seemed to only have questions and no answers—that is, until I met my next patient.

Dr. Jean Pierre was a 67-year-old anthropological pathologist and agnostic who was dying of multiple myeloma, a malignancy that affects the bones, immune system, and kidneys, and the end result of which is renal failure and diffuse skeletal destruction. A commonly seen scenario for patients with this disease includes spinal cord invasion, resulting in paralysis and excruciating bone pain. Dr. Jean Pierre was among the worst cases I'd ever seen.

This highly intelligent and stoic individual had two weeks before his death to describe his life review, as well as the spiritual being that was assisting in this process. Despite his insupportable pain, Dr. Jean Pierre was filled with inner joy as he conveyed his spiritual insights. He described the spiritual entity he called "Michael" as a cosmic, benevolent, and radiant being: "Michael's apparent first order of business, if you will, was to provide the necessary information needed to comprehend my life's lessons so I could transition to the afterlife. God uses familiar images of earthly things to mold our concept of heaven, so that our value of life is outweighed by the overwhelming experience of peace and love. This method allows souls to choose the next world.

"My passion related to the study of humankind and creation, so Michael chose to elucidate God's love, which is the key to understanding our lessons in life, in a way I could identify with. It is this familiar setting that God tailors for each and every soul, to allow for a non-threatening atmosphere where lessons can be reviewed and learned. The key to a joyful and less-convoluted life review is to examine one's actions on a daily basis, and ask God for complete guidance to create the necessary changes that ultimately lead to peace and love. This will allow one to see death as a symbol for a more peaceful and beautiful life. All one has to do is believe in God. That's it! He will do the rest. Despite its simplicity, the preponderance of humans delay to welcome it on their deathbed.

"Dr. Lerma, because I didn't know if God existed, I didn't see death as a positive emotional reaction. This is why Michael was sent to help me attain the yearning to move toward God. I had the angels working overtime to make up for my lackadaisical attitude."

Dr. Jean Pierre said that Michael reached down into his chest and, with a gentle motion, withdrew his spirit. He explained, "My soul was now traversing the universe through a brightly lit tunnel and heading deep into God's heart. I asked Michael if this was a wormhole, the way Einstein had described it, and he said yes.

"Immersed in white light, he began to discuss the importance of spirituality and science with regard to space travel. He said that it may be perfected by scientists in the near future, resulting in both interstellar and intergalactic travel through the use of advanced propulsion systems, amplified gravity, antimatter, and even wormholes. He gave details of meeting other peaceful souls not only in our galaxy, but in the far reaches of the universe. He emphasized that this accomplishment could only be realized if scientists equally persisted in their quest for God. This is imperative, because through spirituality come peace and love. Without these qualities, humans could potentially infect the rest of God's creation with our hatred, pride, and arrogance."

Dr. Jean Pierre asked Michael to enlighten him about free will and how God planned to unfold it. Michael explained to him that grasping the enormity of this divine gift would require traveling back in time to observe the creation of the cosmos and life—life via the first earthly single-celled creature almost four billion years ago, resulting from God's most vast creation more than 13 billion years ago: the universe.

Michael allowed Dr. Jean Pierre to view the enormity of God's fireworks display. He saw God's hand ignite the flame that started it all: the Big Bang. Michael clarified that this supreme act of violence was love in its purest form and that this immense energy assured our existence so humans would have a chance to be co-creators with God. "All this for us?" Dr. Jean Pierre asked Michael. He quoted Michael's response: "All this and infinitely more."

Again Dr. Jean Pierre asked if man would be able to travel throughout the universe one day, and he reported Michael as saying, "Yes, but only when we are not constrained by judgment and objection. All man has to do is have a loving intention for creation and not for destruction. Einstein was nearly on the verge of this acknowledgment but was not given the ability by God, as the world was not ready. After all, look at what politicians did when the power of the atom was discovered: It was not meant to kill others. Had we not taken that route during World War II and not killed so many innocent, spiritual souls, including spiritual scientists, man would already be traversing the galaxy."

Dr. Jean Pierre explained, "Man is continually being given the opportunity to develop cures for fatal illnesses, but not enough scientists and laypeople are praying with fervor and performing acts of unconditional love to allow our needs to transpire. In fact, we are falling prey to our own laws. Just look at the handful of people who have successfully removed prayer from schools. We are not fighting back, because we are too concerned with trying to make money, vanity, and just mere complacency. Despite the millions of people belonging to faith-based churches, only a few are truly praying and carrying out unconditional acts of love and kindness to balance the opposite forces. Just one person praying unconditionally and suffering willingly can raise the level of humanity forever and thus give us the courage to regain our losses. All one has to do is just believe."

Dr. Jean Pierre said that Michael sensed his deep sadness and decided to move to the next lesson, six billion years later. "I found myself back on earth next to a cellular structure I had once seen under the microscope during my early years in college," Dr. Jean Pierre said.

He described the cell as being surrounded by the virginal clear blue waters of the planet left by the melted ice from millions of asteroids and comets: "Angels were flying around the planet, appearing to be guarding God's plan." Dr. Jean Pierre then saw the explosion of life spanning millions of years. He saw nature's first multi-cellular organisms multiplying and then dying. Moving faster than the speed of light, he saw an awesome and frightening sight: several mass extinctions that would appear to decimate nearly every species on the planet. The clear blue oceans were then dark and empty. He said that Michael comforted him by explaining that God's plan, seemingly violent at times, was perfect and best explained through the theory of relativity. Einstein, almost four billion years later, explained that energy is neither created nor destroyed; it only changes form. In other words, Dr. Jean Pierre told me that, because God's plan included love and free will, He thought it would first be introduced by endowing it to the first particles: the atom and its counterparts. "From the very beginning, the atom carried God's immense love and energy needed to explore and love His creation. Thus, the atom-induced mass extinctions were really energies changing form to develop a viable environment for man," Dr. Jean Pierre said. "Slowly, I saw the plants begin to evolve, then insects, only to be lost in the second great mass extinction upon the earth. After that extinction, reptiles were formed independent of the sea, again only to die off. The dinosaurs came into life with flowering plants and the first fish and birds. Their decimation again was required to achieve God's loving plan.

"The time now was about one hundred to two hundred thousand years B.C. I was told that this was when the first *homo sapiens* appeared. The stage had been set. The necessary climate, water, land, plants, trees, and minerals were in place to allow man to live and to create. From cave paintings to the pyramids of Giza to Jesus Christ, Muhammad, Buddha, Da Vinci, Galileo, Columbus, *Apollo 11*, and now a space station, I was shown the natural world as it unfolded.

"As Michael showed me present-day earth, I thought about how it took more than four billion years to create six billion souls, and all from that single cell." Dr. Jean Pierre was told that man could possibly pass, as those before us did, into oblivion, into the sixth extinction that he, as a scientist, knew was already in progress. "Dr. Lerma, I was reassured that God's plan was unfolding in perfection, because it was created out of the greatest ingredient: unconditional love. I was confused about this statement, so I asked Michael how this could occur if man was destroying the environment and each other. I was told that God knew this would occur and was deeply saddened by it; however, He knew this was part of the evolution of free will. When God engineered the planet, He secured its existence through self-protective mechanisms, including tsunamis, hurricanes, volcanoes, and climate changes." Dr. Jean Pierre explained that God wants man to always have access to the planet so as to learn valuable lessons via the human body. He said that the body was engineered to house our soul, to give us the necessary experiences, knowledge, and wisdom to seek and return to God in the hereafter. That is why securing the planet's existence is crucial.

Dr. Jean Pierre told me that he was able to reconcile what he saw with what he had learned on earth. As a scientist, much of what he was shown by Michael was familiar to him and didn't surprise him. However, his knowledge was not able to develop new theories because the spiritual factor or reagent was missing. He understood for the first time that science without God was virtually limited, and that science with God was unlimited. "The S factor," as Dr. Jean Pierre phrased it, "is the missing link and de rigueur to our soul's survival."

By this time, Dr. Jean Pierre was deteriorating rapidly, and he asked if I would pray with him to help him pass from this world to the next. I was honored by his request, and I agreed. Twenty-four hours after our prayer, he looked at me and whispered that Michael and other angels were floating above calling him to follow. He said, "Dr. Lerma, the path the angels are leading me to is so bright and beautiful. The feeling of peace and love is emanating from every single particle of light and penetrating my very soul." He seemed to swiftly focus at the foot of the bed, and, with the most stunning, radiant smile I had ever seen, he took his last breath. I imagined God at the foot of his bed, as many of my other patients had described, washing his feet in humility and pure love as He accepted Dr. Jean Pierre into His heavenly kingdom.

Doctor's Notes
and More Dialogue With Dr. Jean Pierre

The majority of what Dr. Jean Pierre discussed was about the creation of the world and understanding free will. He chose to elaborate on a few other subjects, though, with regard to God's second coming, world peace, hell, and God's unconditional love for all.

Dr. Jean Pierre explained that man will continue to evolve in technology, medicine, and spirituality, because the majority of people on earth are God-loving. As far as total peace on earth, that will occur when man learns to unconditionally love his entire psyche, including his darkest part. Only then will man be able to make a quantum leap toward our heavenly realm here on earth. This event will be preceded by the second visitation of God on earth. During that time, people will develop a faith that can heal one physically and emotionally, and that can move mountains if need be. Technology will involve traveling via teleportation, using gravity machines to distort space and time in order to travel through God's vast universe. Relationships and families will be permanent and loving fixtures here on earth. "This will occur. I saw it in the near future," Dr. Jean Pierre told me.

He went on to say that, whatever we do as souls, we are destined to fail unless we believe and follow the way of Jesus Christ. Michael told Dr. Jean Pierre that God did not want robots to share in His kingdom. He wanted human beings to love Him for Him—as He loved us for us. In other words, we are to desire at our core that which God desires Himself: to love and be loved. That was the impetus for our creation.

Dr. Jean Pierre spoke of God's universal law of homeostasis: For every action, there must be an equal and opposite reaction. He was told that, to achieve nirvana here on earth, one must start by balancing every negative action with a positive one. One can only do this if he or she is genetically healthy and capable (in other words, if one is of sound mind and body). If someone hurts himself or others physically, emotionally, or spiritually, he (or another caring soul) must undertake an act of recompense. Spiritual knowledge and wisdom are needed for this to occur.

Dr. Jean Pierre briefly spoke of sins and the power of forgiveness. He reminded me that Christ died for our sins and that whoever believed in Him would be forgiven and have everlasting life. However, that didn't mean we could continue sinning. That is why consequences exist. They keep most people from repeating the same negative action. Positive actions bring about positive reactions, and vice versa. God did not promise to remove the consequences to our actions; He just promised to forgive us. These consequences act as lessons to make us stronger and more resilient beings. God made sure that every action ultimately leads to a positive one, no matter how horrific the initial action is. Once people can forgive themselves and others, then this world will heal itself.

We will carry our memories into the next realm, possibly the positive and the negative. If one does not forgive himself or herself, the pain of those memories follows. Michael told Dr. Jean Pierre that it hurts God to think that one cannot find forgiveness, because He gave His only Son to the world. All we have to do is believe with all our heart that His Son died for sins past, present, and future. Still, most people do not know the simple truth to everlasting life and love. Their complacency draws them into the raw and powerful forces of darkness, of which pride and guilt are some of the worst.

The good news is that God will never abandon us. He will wait as long as it takes for every soul to seek Him out. After all, He has eternity to work with. Dr. Jean Pierre told me never to forget that energy just changes form and never dies. The same holds true for our soul: It will exist for eternity, and hopefully will not be separated from our loving Creator. In the end, God leaves that up to us. After all, it is about free will.

Dr. Jean Pierre said that hell is definitely a self-separation from God, as God never separates Himself from us. Guilt is the darkest, deepest, and most potent emotion. It can take eons to peel off the layers that are separating the imprisoned soul from experiencing God. Dr. Jean Pierre noted, "I saw people in this state and felt their immeasurable loneliness, self-hatred, fear, and utter coldness. It was horrific."

Michael reminded Dr. Jean Pierre of God's infinite love and how He never ceases from working to set us free from our self-indictment. Dr. Jean Pierre said that he spoke to several people who had been rescued by God. They told him to forgive himself immediately by truly believing that Christ died for our sins. They told him to pray for the millions of souls that choose to remain in pure darkness. "Dr. Lerma, I implore you to pray for those bound souls and tell others to do the same. Work with love and kindness in all you do, every second of every day. Forgive yourself when you fail. Continually pray for self-forgiveness, for the forgiveness of others, and for God's love to live within you and guide all you do, and to set the captives free. Just remember that anything is possible with God. All we have to do is believe."

Conclusion

Dr. Jean-Pierre's comments and the rest of the stories here certainly altered my very essence, leaving me with more questions than answers. As I closed my eyes to ponder about what I had witnessed, I wondered in total awe about our world, its beginning, and its possible end. Was our universe of tangibility and intangibility born of an act of supreme violence, a Big Bang expanding ever outward, a cosmos born of matter and gas 13.7 billion years ago? Who had the audacity for such an idea? Were we part of that plan billions of years ago? Were we here to procreate and replenish the earth before surrendering to our descendants? If there is a beginning, must there be an end? Do we burn as fires in our time, only to be extinguished? Succumbing to the essence of the universe? Will all this end one day? Life no longer passing to life?

As I pictured God's hand, as Dr. Jean Pierre had described, I wondered if He who lit the flame would also let it burn out? Would this lead to our extinction? Or if this fire of life living inside us is meant to go on, who decides? Who will tend the flames? Can our Creator re-ignite the spark even as it turns cold and weak? Is the answer at our death, as we are about to part this world? Is there a plan, a purpose, or a reason to our existence on earth—and after we die? Will we pass, as those before us did, into dark matter, or is the sixth extinction that scientists warn of already in progress? Or will the mystery be revealed through death? A sign? A symbol? A revelation? Or through the physical manifestation of God?

After everything I had seen and heard, how could I believe that this vast universe and the billions of lovingly created souls have no eternal rhyme or reason? These experiences have been no less than life-altering and have literally brought me to my knees in gratitude and unconditional love for our Creator. I believe with all my soul that our spirit energy was not meant to be destroyed or re-created, but to merely change form. The manifestation of this imaginal energy was to experience God's monumental creations. It is quite clear as God's plan continues to unfold that our tears, sadness, and pain will be left with the physical body, only to turn to dust and be cleansed of their iniquities.

The spirits that ultimately connect with God will be left to experience total peace and unconditional love through wisdom and understanding. Those that choose separation will not be forgotten, as God is an all-loving Creator. One's perspective will be vastly different, finally looking at everything with total joy and love, and final understanding of God's awe-inspiring plan. Young Matthew, from Chapter 1, said it best: "God's plan is very difficult to understand now, but soon, you too, and all of God's souls, will play with the dolphins."

Appendix

Evidence for Pre-death Visions of the Afterlife

The quest for facts that support the idea of post-mortem survival and pre-death visions did not appear suddenly. It is rooted as far back as two thousand years ago, when Jesus experienced a pre-death vision that he would be killed and buried, only to rise on the third day. Plato described in *The Republic* the visions of a soldier, Er, who was thought to be killed in action, and the Roman, Pliny the Younger, described a ghost case in Athens where the ghostly information led to the discovery of the bones of a murdered man.

Second-century Palestinian Rabbi Shimon bar Yochai also wrote about pre-death visions, documented in the *Sefer HaZohar* (the "Book of Splendor," often referred to simply as "the Zohar," a five-volume mystical exegesis written in Aramaic on the five books of the Torah). The following is a quote from the Zohar with regard to pre-death visions:

> At the time of a man's death he is allowed to see his relatives and companions from the other world.... [W]e have learned that when a man's soul departs from him, all his relatives and companions in the other world join in and show it the place of delight.... (I, 219a).

The following is a widely reported dream, or pre-death vision, of Abraham Lincoln's, as it was reportedly told to Lincoln's friend, Will Hill Lamon, just days before his assassination:

> There seemed to be a death-like stillness about me. Then I heard subdued sobs, as if a number of people were weeping. I thought I left my bed and wandered downstairs.
>
> I went from room to room.... [T]he same mournful sounds of distress met me as I passed along.... I kept on until I arrived at the East Room, which I entered. There I met with a sickening surprise. Before me was a catafalque, on which rested a corpse.... "Who is dead in the White House?" I demanded of one of the soldiers. "The President" was the answer. "He was killed by an assassin." Then there cam a loud burst of grief from the crowd, which awoke me from my dream. I slept no more that night; and although it was only a dream, I have been strangely annoyed by it ever sense.

In the early 20th century, Sir William Barrett, a physics professor at the Royal College of Science in Dublin and an assistant to the famous physicist John Tyndall, presented research on pre-death experiences in a book entitled *Death-bed Visions* (published in 1926). In 1924, Sir William's wife, an obstetrician, told him about the pre-death account of a young woman who died after delivering her child. As most of my patients described, her dying patient also looked toward the corner of a room with an exhilarating smile, commenting on how beautiful and exalting the spiritual beings were, as well as the world they came from.

The dialogues with the deceased loved ones and heavenly entities were eerily similar with regard to concerns about leaving their living relatives and the strong desire to transition with their deceased loved ones towards the heavenly realm. This sort of negotiation continues until the dying find the comfort needed to transition. Her patient made the decision to depart this world once she knew her newborn child would be cared for.

About 50 years later, Dr. Karlis Osis, Ph.D, director of the American Society for Psychical Research, in New York, continued the systematic survey of deathbed experiences and eventually published his data in a book, *At the Hour of Death*, published in 1977. He surveyed thousands of doctors and nurses present during the final hours of more than 1,000 hospitalized patients. The following are comparisons between Dr. Osis's pilot survey of hospitalized patients in 1961, "Deathbed Observations by Physicians and Nurses," and a 2005 survey I conducted where I interviewed 500-plus hospice patients and their caregivers just hours to days before death:

- In the 1961 survey, four out of five deaths (80 percent) included occurrences of "survival-related" visions (visions that portrayed religious and deceased persons, of which 90 percent of deceased persons were close family members, such as a parent, sibling or child). In the 2005 survey, the number was 85 percent.

- Three out of four people (75 percent) had people coming to take patients to the other side in the 1961 survey, compared with 80 percent in the 2005 survey.

- Forty-one percent of the dying experienced elation and other positive emotions as they died, according to the 1961 survey. The percentage was 90 in the 2005 survey. *Could the large discrepancy be a result of a large number of physicians or nurses with varying views, versus one physician conducting the interviews in the 2005 survey? It is possible that a hospice team resolved patients' issues more timely, thus resulting in greater elation?*

- In the 1961 survey, 29 percent of the dying experienced negative emotions as they died, versus 10 percent in the 2005 survey. *Again, is this likely due to intimate hospice care?*

- Both surveys found that medications and fevers did not relate to the onset of deathbed visions.

- Both surveys found that a patient's sex, age, religion, education, or socioeconomic factors had little or no effect on deathbed visions.

- Both surveys found that hallucinations in the general population mainly consisted of objects, environment, and things, and rarely people; in the terminally ill, the visions were mainly of spiritual beings, deceased loved ones, and a heavenly environment.

- Both surveys found that the duration of visions lasted between one second and five minutes in greater than 80 percent of dying patients. However, patients in the 2005 survey within three days of dying said that at least one angel or spiritual being was in the room at all times. Hours before dying, patients commented that the number of beings increased dramatically, to around 15–20.

❖ The 1961 survey reported that the purpose of spiritual beings was to help patients cross over. The 2005 survey found that spiritual beings or deceased loved ones were coming to aid in patients' life review and that, once understanding was attained, they were guided to the heavenly realm. Those patients actively dying with major unresolved issues or with family member(s) unwilling to accept their death took two to four times longer to depart. Three out of four of these patients died at peace.

❖ Both surveys found that the interval between the first apparitions and death was approximately four weeks.

❖ Both surveys found that the sex of the apparitions were greater than 50 percent male, and approximately 40 percent female. Less than 5 percent reported androgynous beings.

❖ Types of visions and percentage of patients who saw them:
  - God or Jesus (30 percent of patients in both surveys).
  - Angels (24 percent in 1961; 90 percent in 2005).
  - Parents and siblings (20 percent in 1961; 90 percent in 2005).

- Evil beings (3 percent in 1961; 5 percent in 2005).

❧ Both surveys found that greater than 80 percent of patients developed clarity of consciousness with accompanying apparitions, usually three to five days before dying.

One could conclude that these and other trends found in these pilot studies were supportive of the afterlife hypothesis. These results have been further verified, but more research is needed to corroborate the findings with more objective biochemical and radiological parameters. Dr. Bruce Greyson, Director for the Division of Perceptual Studies at the University of Virginia Medical School, is in the process of initiating such a project with hospice patients.

Bibliography

Barrett, W. F. *Death-Bed Visions*. London: Methuen, 1926.

Carr, D. B. "Pathophysiology of Stress-Induced Limbic Lobe Dysfunction: A Hypothesis Relevant to Near-Death Experiences." In B. Greyson and C. P. Flynn, Eds., *The Near-Death Experience: Problems, Prospects, Perspectives*. Springfield, Ill.: Charles C. Thomas, 1984, 125–39.

"Deathbed Observations by Physicians and Nurses: A Cross-Cultural Survey." –*Journal of American Society for Psychical Research*, 71 (1977): 237–59.

Ducasse, C. J. *A Critical Examination of the Belief in a Life After Death*. Springfield, Ill.: Charles C. Thomas, 1961.

Greyson, B., and C. P. Flynn, Eds. *The Near-Death Experience: Problems, Prospects, Perspectives*. Springfield, Ill.: Charles C. Thomas, 1984.

Hart, H. *The Enigma of Survival*. Springfield, Ill.: Charles C. Thomas, 1959.

Huxley, A. *Heaven and Hell*. New York: Harper & Row, 1955.

Kubler-Ross, E. *Death: The Final Stage of Growth*. Englewood Cliffs, N.J.: Prentice-Hall, Inc., 1975.

——. *On Children and Death*. New York: Macmillan Co., 1983.

——. *On Death and Dying*. New York: Macmillan Co., 1969.

Maslow, A. H. *Religions, Values and Peak Experiences*. New York: Viking Press, 1970.

Meredith, Dennis. "Carl Sagan's 'Cosmic Correction' and Extra-Terrestrial Life Wish." *Science Digest*, June 1979.

Moody, R. A. *Life After Life*. Atlanta, Ga.: Mockingbird Books, 1975.

Osis, K. *Deathbed Observations by Physicians and Nurses*. New York: Parapsychology Foundation, Inc., 1961.

Osis, K., and K. Haraldsson. *At the Hour of Death*. New Haven, Conn.: Hastings House, 1997.

Ring, K. *Life at Death. A Scientific Investigation of Near-death Experience*. New York: Coward, McCann and Geoghegan, 1980.

Index

About the Author

J ohn Lerma, M.D., currently serves as a consultant for several hospices and palliative units in Houston and San Antonio, Texas. He is widely known for his compassionate and loving care of hundreds of terminally ill patients, as well as his tenure as the inpatient medical director for the internationally renowned Medical Center Hospice of Houston, Texas. Because the inpatient unit is located in the heart of the largest medical center in the world, he has worked closely with MD Anderson Hospital, the leading cancer institute in the world in research and teaching.

After obtaining a degree in pharmacy at the University of Texas at Austin, he entered medical school at the University of Texas San Antonio and, years later, finished his training in internal medicine. Over the last 10 years he has focused his career in the field of hospice and palliative medicine.

Board-certified in internal medicine as well as hospice and palliative medicine, Dr. Lerma is recognized for his compassionate care of hospice and palliative patients as well as research in the field of pre-death experiences. While working at the Medical Center in Houston, he was involved with teaching hospice and palliative medicine to medical students, residents, and geriatric, oncology and palliative fellows from several institutions. As an international speaker, Dr. Lerma is recognized for his signature lecture, "Pre-Death Experiences: A Hospice Physician's Perspective on Spirituality and the Terminally Ill."

He is a frequent guest of local, national, and international media. Dr. Lerma is creating a non-profit company titled Hearts without Borders, which will take the hospice concept to underserved areas in South America. His organization's current project is to organize a hospice team and travel to several Mexican and South American cities to aid governments and physicians in giving birth to the wonderful gift of hospice.